CONFRONTING GLOBAL WARMING

Health and Disease

CONFRONTING GLOBAL WARMING

Health and Disease

Diane Andrews Henningfeld

Michael E. Mann
Consulting Editor

GREENHAVEN PRESS
A part of Gale, Cengage Learning

GALE
CENGAGE Learning

Detroit • New York • San Francisco • New Haven, Conn • Waterville, Maine • London

GALE
CENGAGE Learning™

Christine Nasso, *Publisher*
Elizabeth Des Chenes, *Managing Editor*

© 2011 Greenhaven Press, a part of Gale, Cengage Learning

For more information, contact:

Greenhaven Press
27500 Drake Rd.
Farmington Hills, MI 48331-3535
Or you can visit our Internet site at
gale.cengage.com.

For product information and technology assistance, contact us at
Gale Customer Support, 1-800-877-4253.

For permission to use material from this text or product, submit all requests online at
www.cengage.com/permissions.

Further permissions questions can be e-mailed to
permissionrequest@cengage.com

Every effort is made to ensure that Greenhaven Press accurately reflects the original intent of the authors. Every effort has been made to trace the owners of copyrighted material.

Cover Image © CDC/PHIL/Corbis.

**LIBRARY OF CONGRESS
CATALOGING-IN-PUBLICATION DATA**

Henningfeld, Diane Andrews.
  Health and disease / Diane Andrews Henningfeld.
    p. cm. -- (Confronting global warming)
  Includes bibliographical references and index.
  ISBN 978-0-7377-4858-1 (hardcover)
  1. Global warming--Health aspects. 2. Climatic changes--Health aspects. 3. Extreme weather--Health aspects. 4. Environmentally induced diseases. 5. Medical climatology. I. Title.
  RA793.H46 2010
  363.738'74--dc22

                          2010014227

Printed in the United States of America
1 2 3 4 5 6 7 14 13 12 11 10

Contents

Preface

> "*The warnings about global warming have been extremely clear for a long time. We are facing a global climate crisis. It is deepening. We are entering a period of consequences.*"
>
> Al Gore

Still hotly debated by some, human-induced global warming is now accepted in the scientific community. Earth's average yearly temperature is getting steadily warmer; sea levels are rising due to melting ice caps; and the resulting impact on ocean life, wildlife, and human life is already evident. The human-induced buildup of greenhouse gases in the atmosphere poses serious and diverse threats to life on earth. As scientists work to develop accurate models to predict the future impact of global warming, researchers, policy makers, and industry leaders are coming to terms with what can be done today to halt and reverse the human contributions to global climate change.

Each volume in the Confronting Global Warming series examines the current and impending challenges the planet faces because of global warming. Several titles focus on a particular aspect of life—such as weather, farming, health, or nature and wildlife—that has been altered by climate change. Consulting the works of leading experts in the field, Confronting Global Warming authors present the current status of those aspects as they have been affected by global warming, highlight key future challenges, examine potential solutions for dealing with the results of climate change, and address the pros and cons of imminent changes and challenges. Other volumes in the series—such as those dedicated to the role of government, the role of industry, and the role of the individual—address the impact various facets of society can have on climate change. The result is a series that provides students and general-interest readers with a solid understanding of the worldwide ramifications of climate change and what can be done to help humanity adapt to changing conditions and mitigate damage.

Each volume includes:

- A descriptive **table of contents** listing subtopics, charts, graphs, maps, and sidebars included in each chapter
- Full-color **charts, graphs, and maps** to illustrate key points, concepts, and theories
- Full-color **photos** that enhance textual material
- **Sidebars** that provide explanations of technical concepts or statistical information, present case studies to illustrate the international impact of global warming, or offer excerpts from primary and secondary documents
- **Pulled quotes** containing key points and statistical figures
- A **glossary** providing users with definitions of important terms
- An annotated **bibliography** of additional books, periodicals, and Web sites for further research
- A detailed **subject index** to allow users to quickly find the information they need

The Confronting Global Warming series provides students and general-interest readers with the information they need to understand the complex issue of climate change. Titles in the series offer users a well-rounded view of global warming, presented in an engaging format. Confronting Global Warming not only provides context for how society has dealt with climate change thus far but also encapsulates debates about how it will confront issues related to climate in the future.

Foreword

Earth's climate is a complex system of interacting natural components. These components include the atmosphere, the ocean, and the continental ice sheets. Living things on earth—or, the biosphere—also constitute an important component of the climate system.

Natural Factors Cause Some of Earth's Warming and Cooling

Numerous factors influence Earth's climate system, some of them natural. For example, the slow drift of continents that takes place over millions of years, a process known as plate tectonics, influences the composition of the atmosphere through its impact on volcanic activity and surface erosion. Another significant factor involves naturally occurring gases in the atmosphere, known as greenhouse gases, which have a warming influence on Earth's surface. Scientists have known about this warming effect for nearly two centuries: These gases absorb outgoing heat energy and direct it back toward the surface. In the absence of this natural greenhouse effect, Earth would be a frozen, and most likely lifeless, planet.

Another natural factor affecting Earth's climate—this one measured on timescales of several millennia—involves cyclical variations in the geometry of Earth's orbit around the sun. These variations alter the distribution of solar radiation over the surface of Earth and are responsible for the coming and going of the ice ages every 100,000 years or so. In addition, small variations in the brightness of the sun drive minor changes in Earth's surface temperature over decades and centuries. Explosive volcanic activity, such as the Mount Pinatubo eruption in the Philippines in 1991, also affects Earth's climate. These eruptions inject highly reflective particles called aerosol into the upper part of the atmosphere, known as the stratosphere, where they can reside for a year or longer. These particles reflect some of the incoming sunlight back into space and cool Earth's surface for years at a time.

Human Progress Puts Pressure on Natural Climate Patterns

Since the dawn of the industrial revolution some two centuries ago, however, humans have become the principal drivers of climate change. The burning of fossil fuels—such as oil, coal, and natural gas—has led to an increase in atmospheric levels of carbon dioxide, a powerful greenhouse gas. And farming practices have led to increased atmospheric levels of methane, another potent greenhouse gas. If humanity continues such activities at the current rate through the end of this century, the concentrations of greenhouse gases in the atmosphere will be higher than they have been for tens of millions of years. It is the unprecedented rate at which we are amplifying the greenhouse effect, warming Earth's surface, and modifying our climate that causes scientists so much concern.

The Role of Scientists in Climate Observation and Projection

Scientists study Earth's climate not just from observation but also from a theoretical perspective. Modern-day climate models successfully reproduce the key features of Earth's climate, including the variations in wind patterns around the globe, the major ocean current systems such as the Gulf Stream, and the seasonal changes in temperature and rainfall associated with Earth's annual revolution around the sun. The models also reproduce some of the more complex natural oscillations of the climate system. Just as the atmosphere displays random day-to-day variability that we term "weather," the climate system produces its own random variations, on timescales of years. One important example is the phenomenon called El Niño, a periodic warming of the eastern tropical Pacific Ocean surface that influences seasonal patterns of temperature and rainfall around the globe. The ability to use models to reproduce the climate's complicated natural oscillatory behavior gives scientists increased confidence that these models are up to the task of mimicking the climate system's response to human impacts.

To that end, scientists have subjected climate models to a number of rigorous tests of their reliability. James Hansen of the NASA Goddard Institute for Space Studies performed a famous experiment back in 1988, when he subjected a climate model (one relatively primitive by modern standards) to possible future fossil fuel emissions scenarios. For the scenario that most closely matches actual emissions since then, the model's predicted course of global temperature increase shows an uncanny correspondence to the actual increase in temperature over the intervening two decades. When Mount Pinatubo erupted in the Philippines in 1991, Hansen performed another famous experiment. Before the volcanic aerosol had an opportunity to influence the climate (it takes several months to spread globally throughout the atmosphere), he took the same climate model and subjected it to the estimated atmospheric aerosol distribution. Over the next two years, actual global average surface temperatures proceeded to cool a little less than 1°C (1.8°F), just as Hansen's model predicted they would.

Given that there is good reason to trust the models, scientists can use them to answer important questions about climate change. One such question weighs the human factors against the natural factors to determine responsibility for the dramatic changes currently taking place in our climate. When driven by natural factors alone, climate models do not reproduce the observed warming of the past century. Only when these models are also driven by human factors—primarily, the increase in greenhouse gas concentrations—do they reproduce the observed warming. Of course, the models are not used just to look at the past. To make projections of future climate change, climate scientists consider various possible scenarios or pathways of future human activity. The earth has warmed roughly 1°C since preindustrial times. In the "business as usual" scenario, where we continue the current course of burning fossil fuel through the twenty-first century, models predict an additional warming anywhere from roughly 2°C to 5°C (3.6°F to 9°F). The models also show that even if we were to stop fossil fuel burning today, we are probably committed to as much as 0.6°C additional warming because of the inertia of the climate system. This inertia ensures warming for a century to come, simply due to our greenhouse gas emissions thus far. This committed warming introduces a profound procrastination penalty for not taking immediate action. If we are to avert an additional warming of 1°C, which would bring the net warming to 2°C—often considered an appropriate threshold for defining dangerous human impact on our climate—we have to act almost immediately.

Long-Term Warming May Bring About Extreme Changes Worldwide

In the "business as usual" emissions scenario, climate change will have an array of substantial impacts on our society and the environment by the end of this century. Patterns of rainfall and drought are projected to shift in such a way that some regions currently stressed for water resources, such as the desert southwest of the United States and the Middle East, are likely to become drier. More intense rainfall events in other regions, such as Europe and the midwestern United States, could lead to increased flooding. Heat waves like the one in Europe in summer 2003, which killed more than 30,000 people, are projected to become far more common. Atlantic hurricanes are likely to reach greater intensities, potentially doing far more damage to coastal infrastructure.

Furthermore, regions such as the Arctic are expected to warm faster than the rest of the globe. Disappearing Arctic sea ice already threatens wildlife, including polar bears and walruses. Given another 2°C warming (3.6°F), a substantial portion of the Greenland ice sheet is likely to melt. This event, combined with other factors, could lead to more than 1 meter (about 3 feet) of sea-level rise by the end of the century. Such a rise in sea level would threaten many American East Coast and Gulf Coast cities, as well as low-lying coastal regions and islands around the world. Food production in tropical regions, already insufficient to meet the needs of some populations, will probably decrease with future warming. The incidence of infectious disease is expected to increase in higher elevations and in latitudes with warming temperatures. In short, the impacts of future climate change are likely to have a devastating impact on society and our environment in the absence of intervention.

Strategies for Confronting Climate Change

Options for dealing with the threats of climate change include both adaptation to inevitable changes and mitigation, or lessening, of those changes that we can still affect. One possible adaptation would be to adjust our agricultural practices to the changing regional patterns of temperature and rainfall. Another would be to build coastal defenses against the inundation from sea-level rise. Only mitigation, however, can prevent the most threatening changes. One means of mitigation that has been given much recent attention is geoengineering. This method involves perturbing the climate system in such a way as to partly or fully offset the warming impact of rising greenhouse gas concentrations. One geoengineering approach involves periodically shooting aerosol particles, similar to ones produced by volcanic eruptions, into the stratosphere—essentially emulating the cooling impact of a major volcanic eruption on an ongoing basis. As with nearly all geoengineering proposals, there are potential perils with this scheme, including an increased tendency for continental drought and the acceleration of stratospheric ozone depletion.

The only foolproof strategy for climate change mitigation is the decrease of greenhouse gas emissions. If we are to avert a dangerous 2°C increase relative to preindustrial times, we will probably need to bring greenhouse gas emissions to a peak within the coming years and reduce them well below current levels within the coming decades. Any strategy for such a reduction of emissions must be international and multipronged, involving greater conservation of energy resources; a shift toward alternative, carbon-free sources of energy; and a coordinated set of governmental policies that encourage responsible corporate and individual practices. Some contrarian voices argue that we cannot afford to take such steps. Actually, given the procrastination penalty of not acting on the climate change problem, what we truly cannot afford is to delay action.

Evidently, the problem of climate change crosses multiple disciplinary boundaries and involves the physical, biological, and social sciences. As an issue facing all of civilization, climate change demands political, economic, and ethical considerations. With the Confronting Global Warming series, Greenhaven Press addresses all of these considerations in an accessible format. In ten thorough volumes, the series covers the full range of climate change impacts (water and ice; extreme weather; population, resources, and conflict; nature and wildlife; farming and food supply; health and disease) and the various essential components of any solution to the climate change problem (energy production and alternative energy; the role of government; the role of industry; and the role of the individual). It is my hope and expectation that this series will become a useful resource for anyone who is curious about not only the nature of the problem but also about what we can do to solve it.

Michael E. Mann

Michael E. Mann is a professor in the Department of Meteorology at Penn State University and director of the Penn State Earth

System Science Center. In 2002 he was selected as one of the fifty leading visionaries in science and technology by Scientific American. *He was a lead author for the "Observed Climate Variability and Change" chapter of the Intergovernmental Panel on Climate Change (IPCC) Third Scientific Assessment Report, and in 2007 he shared the Nobel Peace Prize with other IPCC authors. He is the author of more than 120 peer-reviewed publications, and he recently coauthored the book* Dire Predictions: Understanding Global Warming *with colleague Lee Kump. Mann is also a cofounder and avid contributor to the award-winning science Web site RealClimate.org.*

CHAPTER 1

Health and Disease in a Warming World: An Overview

Over the past several decades, scientists have compiled significant evidence that the planet Earth is undergoing rapid climate change. In particular, meteorologists and climatologists believe that the earth is warming for a variety of reasons. Much of the warming is due to the greenhouse effect. So-called greenhouse gases in the atmosphere trap heat in the lower atmosphere, and protect the planet from the bitter cold of space. As the National Oceanic and Atmospheric Administration (NOAA) notes, "The greenhouse effect is unquestionably real and helps to regulate the temperature of our planet. It is essential for life on Earth and is one of Earth's natural processes."[1]

Why Global Warming Is Alarming

If the greenhouse effect is a natural and necessary process, however, why are so many scientists, government officials, and ordinary citizens alarmed by the prospect of rapid global warming? In the first place, many believe that there is now an excess of greenhouse gases in the atmosphere, and that the buildup will cause excessive heating. Further, there is concern that human beings have altered the natural cycles of the planet through the use of carbon-based fuels such as coal, petroleum, and wood, a phenomenon that has been part of human history only since the industrial revolution in the eighteenth and nineteenth centuries. The twentieth century saw an unprecedented growth in human population and in the demand for carbon-based fuels, and in spite of warnings, the twenty-first-century world shows little sign of being able to control global carbon emissions. NOAA states unequivocally that "human activity has been increasing the concentration of greenhouse gases in the atmosphere (mostly carbon dioxide from combustion of coal, oil, gas . . .). There is no scientific debate on this point." Furthermore, NOAA reports that "seven of the eight warmest years on record have occurred since 2001 and the 10 warmest years have all occurred since 1997. . . . For Northern Hemisphere temperature . . . the warming since the late 19th century is unprecedented over the last 1000 years."[2]

"Climate-sensitive diseases are among the largest global killers. Diarrhoea, malaria and protein-energy malnutrition alone caused more than 3.3 million deaths globally."

But climate change is a very complicated and complex problem. The Pew Center on Global Climate Change reminds people to consider more than just temperature changes, as other climate-related events may affect human life more seriously. They argue that the impacts of climate change have already been observed, including changing weather patterns, water shortages, and rising sea levels, among other events, concluding, "Climate change threatens ecosystems and public health."[3]

Human Health and Global Warming: A Complex Relationship

Human health will indeed be affected by climate change; however, the impacts of global warming interact with each other to either exacerbate or mitigate the threats to human health. As Centers for Disease Control and Prevention (CDC) anthropologist Merrill Singer argues, the threats to health are multifaceted: "Human health is at growing risk due to the multiple climatic effects of global warming. More importantly, it is becoming evident that individual ecocrises are not independent [phenomena], but are intertwined with and contribute to the intensifications of other environmental predicaments."[4] For example, when Hurricane Katrina struck the Gulf Coast of the United States, the initial onslaught, though devastating, turned out not to be the biggest problem. Rather, a combination of environmental damage, insufficient disaster planning, and ineffective protective barriers, among many other factors, worked together to produce one of the worst catastrophes in U.S. history.

Indeed, researchers point to many possibilities for the future health of humankind in a warming world, some of which are positive. For example, far fewer people will be likely to die from exposure to cold temperatures during the winter. In addition, some places will have longer growing seasons, leading to support for human health through good nutrition. Nevertheless, after weighing all the evidence, the Intergovernmental Panel on Climate Change (IPCC), the World Health Organization (WHO), and the Pew Center on Global Climate Change agree that the negative health impacts of climate change around the globe will outnumber the beneficial impacts. Indeed, the WHO asserts, "climate-sensitive diseases are among the largest global killers. Diarrhoea, malaria and protein-energy malnutrition alone caused more than 3.3 million deaths globally in 2002."[5]

The Health Threats of Heat and Drought

Global warming will affect human health both directly and indirectly. The most notable of the direct effects of global warming will be direct temperature effects. As temperatures rise, it is likely that heat waves will increase in frequency, with higher sustained temperatures and longer durations. These factors combine to suggest that more people will die from heat prostration and heat strokes. In addition, the urban heat island effect, a phenomenon created when the dark buildings and pavement of a city raise the temperature of an urban area in comparison to more rural areas, is likely to exacerbate heat waves in cities. In a world that is growing increasingly urban, the health risk to people from direct temperature effects is escalating. The CDC reports, "Studies suggest that, if current emissions hold steady, excess heat-related deaths in the U.S. could climb from an average of about 700 [per] year currently, to between 3,000 and 5,000 per year by 2050."[6]

Scientists also predict that global warming will likely increase the number and severity of droughts. The impact of severe droughts on human health can be devastating on several fronts. In the first place, a lack of rain leads to water shortages. This condition, in turn, leads to lower crop yields and livestock deaths, creating food shortages. When people do not have a wide variety of foods to eat, or not enough food to eat, they are likely to suffer from malnutrition and starvation. Their bodies are also unable to fend off infectious diseases when weakened by hunger.

Drought also leads directly to more and harder-to-control wildfires. In addition to causing a direct threat to human health through burning, wildfires also indirectly affect health through air pollution, the loss of homes and crops, and, at times, forced evacuations.

Extreme Weather: Hurricanes and Floods

While some parts of the world will become drier, other parts of the world will experience excess rain and extremely severe weather, including hurricanes. Hurricanes have the potential of killing or injuring large numbers of people due to high winds; houses can be torn apart, or trees can topple into homes during a storm. In addition, storm surges push many feet of water onto land quickly, destroying everything in the water's path and causing serious flooding. Drowning and injury are likely to occur.

Hurricanes and other storms often produce copious rain as well. In Manila, capital of the Philippines, for example, some 16 inches (40.6 cm) of rain fell in under twelve hours during a tropi-

Hurricane Mitch: A Case Study in Complexity

In 1998, Hurricane Mitch hit Central America. After forming on October 22, 1998, Mitch grew in strength, with winds of 180 miles per hour (290 kph). The storm weakened, however, and by the time it hit Honduras on October 29, 1998, it was only a Category 1 hurricane, packing 80 mph winds (129 kph). Yet Mitch remains the deadliest Atlantic storm since the Great Hurricane of 1780. Mitch killed more than 11,000 people, left more than 3 million people homeless, and left thousands missing. These facts illustrate the complex nature of the interrelationship between climate and human health and provide a picture of the many ways global warming–intensified storms might affect people's lives.

Because Mitch was a slow-moving storm, it dumped a huge amount of rain over the Central American countries of Honduras and Nicaragua—six *feet* (1.8 m) of rain in three days. This extreme weather caused flooding, landslides, and mud slides. Many died in the initial onslaught. Many more died in the weeks, months, and years that followed the storm. Much of the resulting mud was laced with pesticides from large agricultural plantations, contaminating everything it touched. Likewise, the areas around the region's many gold mines became rife with toxic chemicals and heavy metals. Doctors reported that many people suffered from skin and eye diseases as a result. In addition, the contamination of freshwater led to cholera and leptospirosis epidemics, while stagnant water provided ample breeding grounds for mosquitoes carrying malaria and dengue fever, also epidemic in the months after Mitch.

Many people suddenly found themselves refugees, suffering all the health problems associated with this status. In 2009, internationally known public health experts Juan Almendares and Paul R. Epstein noted in "Climate Change and Health Vulnerabilities," in *State of the World 2009: Into a Warming World*, that Honduras continues to suffer economic damage from Mitch. Clearly, the health implications of Mitch demonstrate the complicated, widespread, and long-lasting impact of such storms.

cal storm in September 2009, flooding streets and causing death and injury. Likewise, mudslides are common in rain-soaked mountainous regions where hillsides have been clear-cut for farming. The mud can bury homes and whole villages, as well as the people who live there.

Death and injury from wind and floodwaters are direct threats to human health, but extreme rain events and floods also create many indirect health hazards, including power outages, toxic contamination of water and food supplies, food shortages, and infectious diseases. Molds and fungi can grow in flooded homes, causing residents serious health problems. Many also suffer serious mental health issues in the aftermath of flooding. People who evacuate in the face of severe storms also face threats to health in the form of car accident and the transmission of infectious diseases caused by overcrowded storm shelters.

The Health Threats of Air Pollution and Infectious Disease

Global warming is also predicted to contribute to air pollution. As temperatures increase, so does the incidence of pollutants such as ozone. These pollutants can cause serious lung damage and can worsen cardiovascular disease. In addition, rising temperatures and carbon-dioxide levels caused by global warming will lead to an increase in plant pollens and molds. People suffering from allergies and asthma will suffer impaired health as a result.

Human health will also be threatened by an increasing number of infectious diseases as the planet warms, particularly ones carried by insects and animals. Warmer temperatures mean that insects once confined to the tropics can make their way north. Malaria-carrying mosquitoes, for example, will appear in higher latitudes. Excessive rain and flooding also provide more breeding

Following pages: Heavy rains cause clear-cut hillsides to be less stable, causing mud slides such as this one in Indonesia's Pasir Jambu, West Java, on February 24, 2010. Bay Ismoyo/AFP/ Getty Images.

grounds for insects. In addition, warmer temperatures may extend the life span of certain disease-carrying insects, giving them more time to pass on their diseases to humans. Environmental writer Rebecca Berg contends that the rapid spread of West Nile virus "may be one example of such a disease since . . . a series of warm winters failed to kill some of the mosquito vectors."[7]

Water-borne and food-borne illnesses are likely to increase as well. Bacteria such as salmonella, *E. coli*, and shigella, for example, thrive in humid, warm places. Heavy rains and flooding allow these and other dangerous pathogens to contaminate water supplies. Warmer temperatures also mean that indigenous peoples of the Arctic who prepare their food traditionally and without added refrigeration may find increasing incidence of various kinds of food poisoning, such as botulism and salmonella.

Food and Water: Access and Safety

Global warming will also affect food and water access and safety. As agricultural patterns change due to shifting growing seasons, crop failures may become common in areas that in the past have supported the human population. Although the warm temperatures may extend the growing season and actually provide more food in some areas, in others, drought will destroy crops before they reach maturity. Flooding in other places will deplete soil nutrients and damage agriculture. In either case, malnutrition and starvation are possible.

Food safety becomes an issue during climate change as well. As the climate warms, food contamination becomes more common, both in home storage and in industrial settings. This is because bacteria such as salmonella and *E. coli* thrive and multiply at warmer temperatures. Keeping equipment very clean can help; in addition, cold foods must be kept cold to retard bacterial growth, and hot foods must be thoroughly cooked to kill contaminating bacteria. Therefore, food manufacturers will need to take extra precautions, such as scrupulous attention to cleanliness and storage temperatures of food to ensure their products do not cause illnesses or deaths. In addition, more pests such as insects and rodents will thrive in warmer temperatures, increasing the likelihood that they will contaminate food.

Water safety and access, like food security and safety, is another essential element for human life. Global warming will likely have a negative impact on fresh water availability and safety in areas where there is too much water, such as in flooding and storms, and in areas where there is not enough water, such as drought-stricken regions. Even as more water will be needed—for humans, animals, and crops—to cope with rising temperatures, less water may be available.

The Health Effects of Rising Sea Levels and Melting Ice

Melting ice sheets and rising sea levels also negatively affect large numbers of people around the world. In the Arctic, indigenous peoples may find their traditional cultures disappearing. They may contract fatal diseases from their traditional methods of food preparation. In addition, they stand a greater chance of drowning while hunting and fishing as the ice melts and breaks apart. Their traditional food sources will experience a loss of habitat as well, leading to less available food.

Additionally, rising sea levels mean that many islands in the world will be under water. The WHO warns that islands such as the Maldives, the Marshall Islands, and Tuvalu are at risk. People who call the islands home will be forced to migrate, suffering the health deterioration that often accompanies refugee status. As senior fellow and director of climate strategy at the American Progress Fund Daniel J. Weiss and colleague Robin Pam argue, "With displacement comes increased transmission of waterborne disease from stagnant water, the challenge of feeding and sheltering the displaced, sewage backups and squalid conditions, and strained disaster relief resources."[8]

In addition, coastal areas will experience increased flooding and be at even greater jeopardy from storm surges. Because nearly

THE RELATIONSHIP BETWEEN CLIMATE CHANGE AND HEALTH

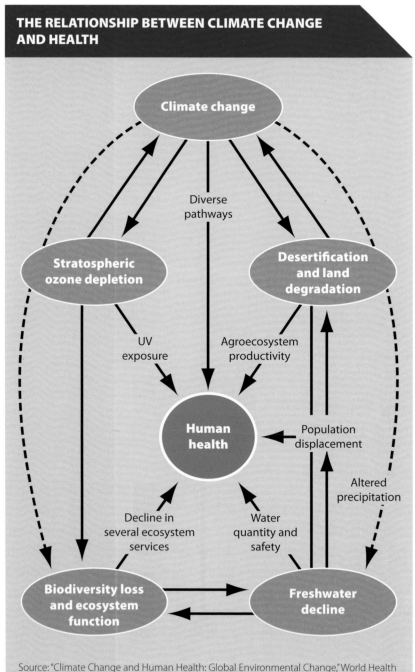

Climate change

Diverse
pathways

Stratospheric
ozone depletion

Desertification
and land
degradation

UV
exposure

Agroecosystem
productivity

Human
health

Population
displacement

Altered
precipitation

Decline in
several ecosystem
services

Water
quantity and
safety

Biodiversity loss
and ecosystem
function

Freshwater
decline

Source: "Climate Change and Human Health: Global Environmental Change," World Health Organization, 2009. www.who.int/globalchange/ecosystems/en.

half the world's population lives in coastal, low-lying areas, many people may drown or lose their homes. In addition, they will be subject to all the diseases rampant in flooded areas, including cholera. Weiss and Pam note that the most susceptible areas are "densely populated river deltas and coastal cities in Asia."[9]

Finally, rising sea levels may mean that coastal areas will suffer from the incursion of seawater in freshwater reservoirs and on land. Such encroachment poses serious threats to human health. First, an incursion of seawater will make freshwater undrinkable. Second, when seawater floods land traditionally used for farming, the ocean's salt content makes the land unsuitable for crops. Finally, if seawater incursion occurs in rivers, it will kill all freshwater fish and other food sources.

Preparing for a Warmer World

Although the impact of global warming on human health is largely negative, there are many ways that people, governments, businesses, and institutions can prepare themselves. With careful planning and preparation, many of the health risks can be lessened or avoided altogether. Because the poorest people of the world will suffer the greatest consequences from global warming—though they have contributed the least to the release of greenhouse gasses—it is important for wealthier nations to consider the responsibility they bear for all the people of the world. In the chapters that follow, the health risks mentioned above will be examined in greater detail, as well as ways that the risks can be mitigated. Working together, people can shoulder many of the challenges global warming places on health.

Notes

1. "Global Warming: Frequently Asked Questions," National Oceanic and Atmospheric Administration, August 20, 2008. www.ncdc.noaa.gov.
2. "Global Warming: Frequently Asked Questions."
3. "Climate Change 101: Science and Impacts," *Climate Change 101: Understanding and Responding to Global Climate Change*, Pew Center on Global Climate Change, January 2009. www.pewclimate.org.

4. Merrill Singer, "Beyond Global Warming: Interacting Ecocrises and the Critical Anthropology of Health," *Anthropological Quarterly*, vol. 82, Summer 2009, p. 795.
5. "Climate and Health," Fact Sheet No. 266, World Health Organization, August 2007. www.who.org.
6. "Health Effects," *Climate Change and Public Health*, U.S. Centers for Disease Control and Prevention, 2009. www.cdc.gov.
7. Rebecca Berg, "The Future of Children's Environmental Health: Coping with Global Warming," *Journal of Environmental Health*, vol. 71, October 2008, pp. 56–58.
8. Daniel J. Weiss and Robin Pam, "The Human Side of Global Warming," Center for American Progress, April 10, 2008. www.americanprogress.org.
9. Weiss and Pam, "The Human Side of Global Warming."

CHAPTER 2

The Direct Temperature Effects of Global Warming on Health

Human beings have remarkable adaptability for surviving temperature extremes. Many people live in marginal areas where they will encounter either very hot or very cold conditions. The !Kung people who live in the Kalahari Desert in the African countries of Botswana, Namibia, and South Africa, for example, show a very high degree of heat tolerance. Likewise, the Inuit people who live in the Arctic have adapted to extremely cold temperatures. Nonetheless, as Mark Maslin, director of the Environment Institute at University College London writes, "Although it is clear that humanity can live, survive, and even flourish from the Arctic to the Sahara, what causes problems is when the predictable extremes of local climate are exceeded."[1]

The Effects of Extreme Temperatures on Human Health

According to the Canadian Center for Occupational Health and Safety, most people feel comfortable when the thermometer reads between 68° to 80°F (20° to 27°C). At higher temperatures, people begin to experience the symptoms of heat stress, particularly if the humidity is also high, a circumstance that impairs the body's ability to cool itself. Similarly, according to the same source, when temperatures fall below the comfort level, and people do not wear protective clothing, they can experience a drop in their core temperature, which normally hovers around 98.6°F (37°C) for most humans. Exposure to extreme cold without adequate covering and a concurrent drop in the body's core temperature can result in mild to severe hypothermia and death. In addition, when people are wet, their tolerance to cold is greatly reduced, as moisture conducts heat away from the body.

When temperatures reach extreme or historic levels, either hot or cold, human death and illness increase, especially the longer the extreme temperatures last. Indeed, human mortality rates due to temperature extremes can be placed on a graph that will produce a U-shaped curve: More human deaths and illnesses occur at temperature extremes. In addition, the number of deaths increases dramatically with each degree as cold temperatures fall and hot temperatures rise.

Severe Heat Waves Are Increasing

Global warming models suggest that there will be an increase in the frequency of severe heat waves over the next decades. According to the Pew Center on Global Climate Change, "Average temperatures are rising, but extreme temperatures are rising even more: In recent decades hot days and nights have grown more frequent, cold days and nights less frequent. There have been more frequent heat waves and hotter high temperature extremes."[2]

A heat wave is simply a period of time in which the daily mean temperature rises significantly above the expected temperature for the season. The Centers for Disease Control and Prevention (CDC) define an "extreme heat event" as one in which there are "several days of temperatures greater than 90°F; warm, stagnant air masses; and consecutive nights with higher-than-usual minimum temperatures."[3]

Obviously, these conditions pose a particular danger in the summer, when the average mean daily temperature is already hot in many parts of the world. Heat waves are classified as mild, moderate, and severe. Severe heat waves maintain higher sustained temperatures over longer periods of time. With time, the body's ability to tolerate heat declines rapidly.

The Quiet Catastrophe:
The European Heat Wave of 2003

Unlike Hurricane Katrina, a storm that slammed into the Gulf Coast of the United States in 2005, killing hundreds of Louisiana and Mississippi residents in its wake, the European heat wave of 2003 arrived unannounced and silently began killing thousands of Italians, French, Portuguese, Swiss, Germans, British, Belgians, Spanish, and other Europeans over a period of weeks. By the time the heat passed, Europe had endured its hottest summer temperatures in more than 500 years.

Initially, the United Nations estimated that the heat wave killed some 30,000 people, making it the worst natural disaster in 50 years. More accurate accounts in the years following the event, however, made it clear that more than 52,000 Europeans perished as a result of the heat wave. The heat wave of 2003 now stands as one of the deadliest natural catastrophes in European history. Its silence made it no less dangerous than the most violent earthquake or tornado.

Writing in *Nature* in 2004, Peter Stott and his colleagues from the Hadley Centre for Climate, Prediction, and Research, and from Oxford University, stop just short of blaming the European catastrophe of 2003 on global warming. Nonetheless, they project that during the next forty years, devastating heat waves such as the one in 2003 are likely to increase hundred-fold. These increases, the researchers assert, will be the result of anthropogenic (human-caused) climate change.

Currently, extreme cold snaps cause more deaths than do heat waves. At the same time, however, the number of cold-related deaths seems to be declining. This shift may be in part because improved housing and heating protect more people against the cold. Additionally, scientists have projected that cold-related deaths may drop as a result of global warming. It is also possible that the increased number of deaths due to heat events may more than offset the reduction in deaths due to cold, however, leading to a net increase in the number of direct temperature-related deaths overall.

Heat Waves and Human Mortality and Morbidity

The Intergovernmental Panel on Climate Change (IPCC) revealed in a 2007 report written by Brazilian professor of public health Ulisses Confalonieri and colleagues that "hot days, hot nights, and heat waves have become more frequent. . . . Heat waves are associated with marked short-term increases in mortality."[4] Human mortality and morbidity, that is, the rate of death and illness in a given human population, due to heat comes generally from two sources: heat exhaustion and heat strokes; and coronary disease and strokes.

Heat exhaustion is the most common human illness related to heat exposure. The symptoms are initially mild, according to the National Center for Environmental Health's George Luber

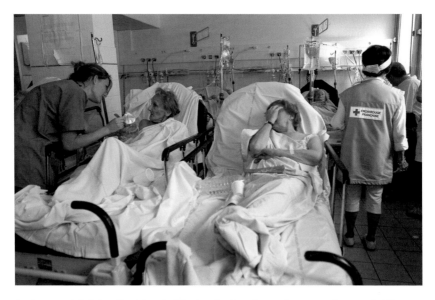

Patients await help in a Paris hospital during the 2003 August heat wave that scorched Europe, killing as many as fifty-two thousand people. Jean Ayissi/AFP/Getty Images.

and Michael McGeehin, writing in the *American Journal of Preventive Medicine* in 2008. They include dizziness, fainting, vomiting, excessive sweating, and thirst, among other symptoms. Although the skin may feel cool and moist, and the body's core temperature remains normal, these symptoms, if ignored, can lead to the far more serious condition, heat stroke.

"[Heat waves] account for more deaths annually than hurricanes, tornadoes, floods, and earthquakes combined."

The severity of heat stroke cannot be overestimated. Someone suffering from heat exhaustion can quickly move into heat stroke, at which point the body's core temperature spikes to greater than 105°F (40.6°C), according to Luber and McGeehin. The symptoms of heat stroke include convulsions and coma; people suffering from this condition often die. What makes people particularly vulnerable to heat stroke during a heat wave is that evening temperatures do not drop enough for the person's body to sufficiently cool off overnight, and the effects of heat exposure are cumulative. Thus, people living in housing without air conditioning or other cooling technologies, especially the elderly and the young, are at great risk during a prolonged heat wave.

In addition, extended heat waves increase the number of deaths caused by cardiovascular diseases such as heart attacks and strokes and by respiratory disease, according to studies cited by Luber and McGeehin. These deaths are not always attributed to a heat wave, however. As Luber and McGeehin argue, "Because heat-related illnesses can cause various symptoms and exacerbate a wide variety of existing medical conditions, the etiology can be difficult to establish when the illness onset or death is not witnessed by a physician."[5] That is, it is difficult for doctors to determine the underlying cause of death when a patient presents with a heart attack or stroke, as these conditions are often made worse by heat waves. In addition, heat exhaustion and heat stroke are not diseases that doctors are required to report to public health organizations. Therefore, although heat waves "account for more deaths annually than hurricanes, tornadoes, floods, and earthquakes combined,"[6] according to the CDC, the number of deaths *attributed* to heat waves may still be greatly lower than the *actual* count.

The Danger of Heat Waves and the Urban Heat Island for Aging Populations

Increasingly, the human population of the world is living in urban areas. This fact is ominous for the toll heat waves may take in the coming decades. Cities often create their own environment, known as a heat island. According to the City Arborist Program in Austin, Texas, the heat island effect can raise temperatures from 2° to 9°F (about 5°C) in cities.

There are several reasons for this phenomenon. In urban areas, particularly those with large populations, there is less vegetation than one would find in a more rural area. Trees and plants help to offset extreme heat by two mechanisms. First, trees and vegetation provide shade for buildings, thus keeping them cooler and allowing air conditioners to work more efficiently. Second, according to the U.S. Environmental Protection Agency (EPA), trees and vegetation cool the air through the process of evapotranspiration. In this process, trees absorb water through their roots and then give off water vapor through their leaves by the process of evaporation, a process that uses up some of the stored heat in the atmosphere. With fewer trees and plants in an urban setting, cities become even hotter than rural areas do during a heat wave.

A second cause of the urban heat island effect is the increase in impervious land covers such as concrete parking lots, buildings, and roads. These structures prevent rainwater from soaking into the soil and then later evaporating, a process that cools the atmosphere. Rather, the rainwater runs off the impervious areas

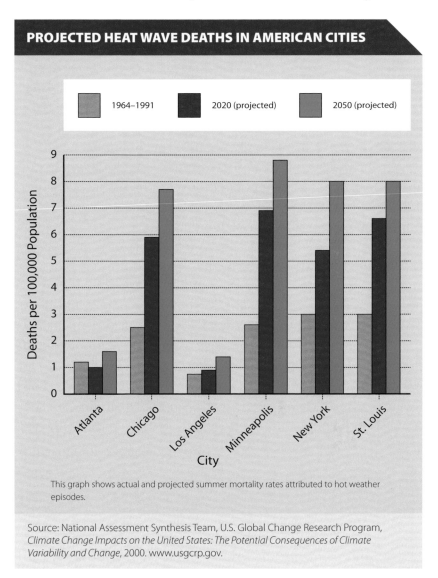

PROJECTED HEAT WAVE DEATHS IN AMERICAN CITIES

Legend: 1964–1991 | 2020 (projected) | 2050 (projected)

Y-axis: Deaths per 100,000 Population

X-axis: City — Atlanta, Chicago, Los Angeles, Minneapolis, New York, St. Louis

This graph shows actual and projected summer mortality rates attributed to hot weather episodes.

Source: National Assessment Synthesis Team, U.S. Global Change Research Program, *Climate Change Impacts on the United States: The Potential Consequences of Climate Variability and Change*, 2000. www.usgcrp.gov.

quickly and goes into city storm drains, instead of soaking into the ground.

Finally, cities also produce a lot of carbon dioxide from the large number of cars and industries located there. Carbon dioxide is a greenhouse gas, one that traps heat near the surface of the earth rather than letting it escape into the upper atmosphere.

For these reasons, the urban heat island effect can turn a moderate heat wave into a life-threatening event for city dwellers. With an increasing number of extreme heat events forecast as the result of global warming, it is likely that the urban heat island effect will play an increasingly negative role in human health.

The health impact of an increasing number of heat waves is also exacerbated by aging populations. In much of northern Europe, North America, and Japan, the median age of the population is increasing. Public health officials have long known that the individuals most vulnerable to the effects of heat exposure are the elderly and the very young. According to Confalonieri and colleagues, "Increasing the number of older adults in the population will increase the proportion of the population at risk because a decreased ability to thermoregulate is a normal part of the aging process."[7] That is, because older adults cannot regulate their body temperatures as effectively as younger people, they are much more vulnerable to the dangerous effects of heat. When the percentage of elderly in a population rises, therefore, the percentage of the population vulnerable to illness or death by heat exposure rises concurrently.

Mitigating the Dangers of Extreme Heat Events

In 2003, Europe suffered a terrible heat wave that resulted in as many as 52,000 deaths. As a result, the French government put into place a series of interventions that has proved successful in saving lives since then. These include health-warning systems and the establishment of cool shelters where people can go to reduce their body temperatures. Other governments have followed suit. Maslin reports that "the population in Europe has successfully adapted [its] lifestyle to take into consideration the high summer temperatures. This is a classic case of individual risk assessment and adaptation."[8] Likewise, in the United States, the

CDC has established a series of strategies to help prevent death and illness in the event of extreme heat events. These include the following:

- Checking on elderly and homebound neighbors during heat waves
- Reducing strenuous activities
- Dressing in lightweight and light-colored clothing
- Increasing access to air-conditioned spaces

Although the health risks associated with the direct temperature effects of global warming are serious, and though they can cause long-term illnesses and death, public health officials are working hard to prepare for the increased number of heat waves predicted by virtually every model of the future. Nevertheless, the CDC reports, "Studies suggest that, if current emissions hold steady, excess heat-related deaths in the U.S. could climb from an average of about 700 each year currently, to between 3,000 and 5,000 per year by 2050."[9] Protecting the most vulnerable members of the population, therefore, has become a vital concern.

Notes

1. Mark Maslin, *Global Warming: A Very Short Introduction*. Oxford: Oxford University Press, 2004, pp. 83–84.
2. "Climate Change 101: Science and Impacts," *Climate Change 101: Understanding and Responding to Global Climate Change*, Pew Center on Global Climate Change, January 2009. www.pewclimate.org.
3. "Health Effects," *Climate Change and Public Health*, U.S. Centers for Disease Control and Prevention. www.cdc.gov.
4. Ulisses Confalonieri et al., "2007: Human Health," *Climate Change 2007: Impacts, Adaptation and Vulnerability. Contribution of Working Group II to the Fourth Assessment Report of the Intergovernmental Panel on Climate Change*, eds. M.L. Perry et al. Cambridge: Cambridge University Press, 2007, pp. 396–97.
5. George Luber and Michael McGeehin, "Climate Change and Extreme Heat Events," *American Journal of Preventive Medicine*, vol. 35, November 2008, p. 430.
6. "Health Effects," CDC.
7. Confalonieri et al., "2007: Human Health," p. 408.
8. Maslin, *Global Warming*, p. 94.
9. "Health Effects," CDC.

CHAPTER 3

Aridity and Human Health: Drought, Desertification, and Wildfires

One of the most devastating threats to human health derives from a lack of adequate rainfall. Without rain, farmers cannot raise their crops. Without rain, livestock cannot survive. Without rain, land that was formerly lush and rich, providing healthy habitats for people, plants, and animals, dries up, becomes dust, and blows away.

Drought and Desertification: Threats to Health

Scientists use the word "drought" to describe a condition when an area or region receives less rain than would be expected over a significant amount of time, long enough that the lack of rain results in serious destruction to crops and water supplies. Over time, drought can lead to severe malnutrition, famine, and death by starvation or opportunistic infections that take advantage of bodies weakened by hunger.

Most climatologists agree that not only will the world become warmer in the coming decades, many parts of the world will suffer from extreme drought. In 2006, the British Met Office, the official weather forecasting bureau in the United Kingdom, projected a rise of between 2.3°F to 7.4°F (1.3°C to 4.2°C) by the end of the century. Such an increase in temperature would double the incidence of moderate drought and also increase the frequency of extreme droughts.

Drought can leave people—like this Indonesian farmer, who stands in his ruined rice paddy— without their regular food sources. AP Images.

Worse, more than two billion people in the world live in what are called drylands, places where rainfall is barely adequate to sustain human life. When these areas experience drought conditions, they can quickly revert to deserts in a process known as desertification. As humans attempt to eke out livelihoods in areas undergoing desertification, they often engage in practices that exacerbate, rather than aid, the situation. For example, farmers may attempt to plow more land in order to plant more crops to make up for the low crop yields. Plowing arid land and exposing the soil to hot, windy conditions causes dust storms and rapid desertification, however. Again, the degradation of farm and pasture lands makes it difficult to raise crops and keep livestock. This, in turn, often leads to malnutrition, famine, and death by starvation or opportunistic infections.

Even in areas that are not normally arid, drought can occur when rainfall does not come as expected. The Pew Center on Global Climate Change predicts, "As the atmosphere becomes

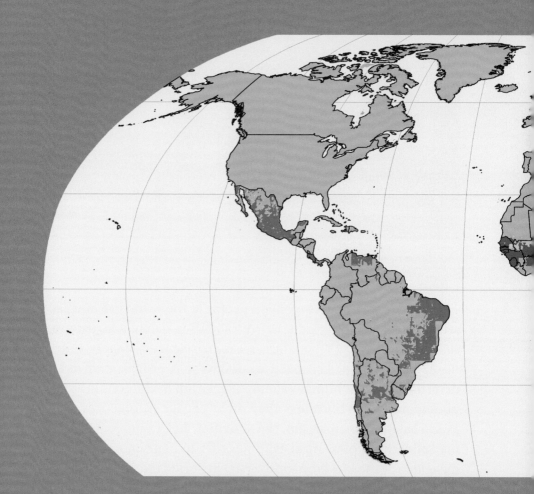

Source: Center for Hazards and Risk Research The Earth Institute at Columbia University, *Natural Disaster Hotspots: A Global Risk Analysis*, March 29, 2005. www.ldeo.columbia.edu.

Drought Mortality Risk

Medium

High

Extreme

warmer, it can hold more water, increasing the length of time between rain events and the amount of rainfall in an individual event. So, even areas where the average annual rainfall *increases* [emphasis added] may experience more frequent and longer droughts."[1] Because of this factor, as the planet warms, rains might not fall when they are needed to nurture crops. When the rains come, however, they may be excessive, leading to flooding and further destruction of homes and farmlands.

For example, as Worldwatch Institute senior researcher Brian Halweil reports, "Asian farmers . . . are facing their own climate-related problems. In the unirrigated rice paddies and wheat fields of Asia, the annual monsoon can make or break millions of lives. Yet the reliability of the monsoon is increasingly in doubt."[2]

"In Africa, drought is the single most important natural hazard in terms of shattered livelihoods, starvation, deaths, and nutrition-related diseases."

Monsoons, those seasonal shifts in wind direction that usually bring with them rainfall, are affected by El Niño events, a cycle of warming that occurs in the eastern Pacific Ocean. In El Niño years, the monsoons are weak and do not produce the rain that people depend on for their livelihoods. It is predicted that El Niño events will occur more often in coming years because of global warming. This change, in turn, will trigger drought and crop failures, directly affecting the health of millions of people. Halweil describes just such a situation that occurred in Indonesia in 1997. In that year, Indonesia suffered an El Niño–induced drought, leading to huge food losses. The drought was broken by a very wet winter that caused additional suffering because planting could not be started on time, and rats and locusts flourished, destroying both crops and stored food supplies. Halweil, citing Bambang Irawan of the Indonesian Center for Agricultural Socio-Economic Research and Development, notes that "this succession of poor harvests forced many families to eat less rice and turn to the less nutritious alternative of dried cassava."[3]

Drought: The Precursor to Malnutrition and Famine

Although drought is not the same as famine, it contributes to the development of famine conditions over time. Jonatan Lassa, the coordinator of the Dutch relief organization HIVOS, argues that famine is "both a slow developing disaster and a process."[4] Long before people begin to die of starvation, drought begins to affect the health of people living in arid lands. The first stage in the process is crop failure and low yields. Serious food shortages and skyrocketing food prices follow. Poorer people begin to cut back on their food intake, and they also cut back on food diversity by choosing cheaper foods that fill the belly, even if such foods do not provide sufficient nutrition. Brazilian professor of public health Ulisses Confalonieri and his colleagues identify some of the health effects of drought caused by global warming: "Both acute and chronic nutritional problems are associated with climate variability and change. The effects of drought on health include deaths, malnutrition (undernutrition, protein-energy malnutrition and/or micronutrient deficiencies), infectious diseases and respiratory diseases."[5] A reduction in food consumption results in undernutrition. Protein-energy malnutrition means that there is insufficient intake of protein, from either plant or animal sources. Finally, micronutrient deficiencies mean that the body is suffering from a lack of important nutrients, found in a variety of foods. For example, inadequate thiamine (vitamin B_1) leads to the nervous disorder beriberi. Any and all of these conditions happen amid diminished dietary diversity—that is, when people are unable to obtain a wide variety of foods, they become malnourished in one or more ways.

Drought is particularly dangerous in Africa, where more than 43 percent of the terrain consists of arid lands, according to Kenyan journalist Peter Mwaura. "In recent years," Mwaura writes, "drought-related famine has killed more people in Africa than in any other continent. . . . In Africa, drought is the single most important natural hazard in terms of shattered livelihoods, starvation, deaths, and nutrition-related diseases."[6]

If a drought is short-lived, people and regions recover fairly quickly. When droughts extend over years, however, problems multiply rapidly. People who are subjected to chronic malnutrition are much more susceptible to infectious diseases, as well as nutrition-related diseases. Moreover, as Confalonieri notes, "A study in southern Africa suggests that HIV/AIDS amplifies the effect of drought on nutrition."[7] Thus, a deadly cycle emerges: People who are malnourished do not have the strength to fight off diseases, and anyone already infected with serious disease is more likely to become malnourished in times of drought.

Drought, Dust Storms, and Health

Drought is not limited to Africa and Asia, however. Researchers from the Lamont-Doherty Earth Observatory of Columbia University, led by Richard Seager, state bluntly, "projections of anthropogenic [human-caused] climate change show widespread agreement that Southwestern North America—and the subtropics in general—are on a trajectory to a climate even more arid than now." As a result of his research, Seager predicts that the Southwest will soon enter a period of "perpetual drought."[8] Although people who live in such areas in the developed world may not find themselves in danger of starvation, it is likely that their lives will be disrupted by the inability of the land to support human habitation.

It is also likely that some people will be exposed to another serious health risk: dust storms. In the United States during the 1930s, record droughts over a period of three years turned the middle part of the country into what has been called the Dust Bowl. Plowed land, desiccated by searing temperatures and howling winds, turned to dust and blew across the country, blackening out the sun and covering everything with dirt. People who lived in this area, many of them too poor to move away, endured days when they were unable to leave their homes. Many people breathed in the fine dust and were afflicted by an often-fatal disease known as Dust Bowl pneumonia.

Residents of eastern Australia experienced firsthand the consequences of a dust storm in September 2009. Gale-force winds drove dust from drought-stricken New South Wales through Sydney, Australia's largest city. Many experienced difficulty with breathing, even those who remained indoors.

Global Warming, Drought, and Wildfires

Although famine and malnutrition tend to be the most dangerous health consequences of drought in poorer countries, there is another significant health hazard engendered by global warming and drought across the globe, including North America, Europe, and Australia. No less a body than the Nobel Prize–winning Intergovernmental Panel on Climate Change has stated with very high confidence that "a warming climate encourages wildfires through a longer summer period that dries fuels, promoting easier ignition and faster spread."[9] Likewise, a research team led by University of Oregon professor J.R. Marlon notes, "It is widely accepted, based on data from the last few decades and on model simulations, that anthropogenic [human-caused] climate change will cause increased fire activity."[10]

Some of the negative health effects of wildfire are obvious: fast-moving flames, racing across tinder-box-dry vegetation and fanned by winds, can quickly engulf people and animals, leading to serious injury or death from burning. On February 7, 2009, for example, southeastern Australia suffered through some of the worst firestorms in that country's history. Indeed, science writer Ken Eastwood notes, "climatologists agree that it was climate change that made the February fires Australia's worst peacetime disasters. As well as suffering a decade-long drought . . . Victoria

Greece on Fire

In the summer of 2007, massive forest fires broke out across Greece. The country had suffered through three heat waves during which the temperatures topped 100°F (37.8°C), even reaching a record-breaking 113°F (45°C) in July. In addition, a severe drought gripped the country. These conditions, predicted by models of global warming, made the forests vulnerable to human carelessness or arson. One match, and the countryside would be in flames.

More than three thousand fires raged across Greece in the hot, dry summer of 2007, not dying down until September. By the time the last flames were put out in early September, sixty-seven people had died, including several firefighters. Others had been injured, and many lost their homes and their livelihoods. An additional health impact of the fiery summer was the pall of smoke that hung in the air, making breathing difficult for all and dangerous for those with medical conditions.

Although the conditions in the summer of 2007 were unprecedented, the fires returned in August 2009. No one died in the 2009 round, but the capital city of Athens was threatened. Gale-force winds fanned the flames, and for a time, it appeared that the city that gave birth to classical Greek civilization thousands of years ago might not survive the summer of 2009.

If the models hold true, and the predictions of climatologists come to pass, wildfires will continue to rage out of control across southern Europe, posing serious danger to the health of people in Greece and elsewhere.

had a heat wave in the days and weeks leading up to 7 February that broke nearly every temperature record in the book."[11]

By the time the Australian fires had burned themselves out, more than 200 people were dead, many of them engulfed by flames they had no time to escape. Although many had fire plans in place, the fires spread so quickly that no precautions could save them. More than 1,800 homes were destroyed, according to

Eastwood, and whole towns were nothing more than rubble after the fires' passing. He cites David Karoly, a meteorologist at the University of Melbourne, who predicts that there will be a 100 percent increase in the frequency of such fires.

Other health risks posed by wildfire are less dramatic but nonetheless potent. A study by atmospheric scientists at Harvard University and reported by the American Geophysical Union predicts that by 2055, "wildfires in the western United States could scorch about 50 percent more land than they do now, causing a sharp decline in the region's air quality."[12] The increase in smoke and suspended particles in the air will cause serious breathing difficulty for those whose breathing is already impaired, such as individuals who suffer from asthma, chronic bronchitis, and cardiovascular disease.

In 2007, James M. Seltzer and his colleagues at the Pediatric Environmental Health Specialty Units of the University of California, Irvine, released a statement concerning the health risks of wildfires for children in particular. They noted that both fire and smoke are serious dangers. They also addressed the byproducts of burning wood, plastics, and chemicals as components of the smoke. The doctors argue that, because children have smaller lungs than adults, youngsters are especially vulnerable to smoke-related injury. In addition, the report also addressed the extreme psychological stress a wildfire can place on children.

Coping with the Effects of Drought, Aridity, and Wildfires

Daniel Sarewitz, the director of Arizona State University's Consortium for Science, Policy, and Outcomes, is among many who believe that nations and people must adapt to climate change, including drought, in order to survive, rather than focusing solely on mitigating global warming. Likewise, the U.S. Environmental Protection Agency admits that "some degree of future climate change will occur regardless of future greenhouse gas emissions."[13]

Thus, though drought, aridity, and wildfires pose significant health risks to much of the world's population, there are steps that can be taken to limit the damage. Governments can establish drought management strategies that include purchasing and storing food supplies so that in time of drought, people need not starve. In addition, governments can establish water reservoirs and plans for water distribution. In both cases, however, care must be taken to ensure that the coping strategy does not cause other serious health problems.

For example, in a 2007 article from the World Watch Institute, "Climate Change Coming Home: Global Warming's Effects on Populations," science writer Sarah De Weerdt tells the story of how one government's effort to increase crop yields during a time of drought led to more health woes for the region's inhabitants. In Ethiopia's Tigray region, little rain has fallen since the 1970s, leading to sporadic malnutrition and full-blown famine. In an attempt to address the issue, the government built a series of dams that helped to collect what rain fell, and then to divert the rainwater for use in irrigating fields. The project was initially deemed a success; crop yields increased and hunger was assuaged. Many children began to suffer from malaria, however, a mosquito-borne illness. Researchers soon discovered that the stored water behind the dams provided a perfect breeding ground for malaria-carrying mosquitoes. This example is not to suggest that governments, industry, and private individuals should not explore mitigation and adaptation ideas; rather, that any idea to be implemented ought to be well researched and planned.

Important strategies include educating farmers and citizens about what practices increase the risk of soil loss and dust storms. Some farming techniques can help to preserve the soil rather than leaving it vulnerable to the elements. In addition, planting drought-resistant crops and altering planting cycles to respond to changing weather patterns could increase crop yields and stave off the most serious episodes of malnutrition and famine.

Vigorous fire management plans must be in place in areas where wildfires are likely. Health officials must be prepared to treat people who experience smoke inhalation during wildfire seasons. Perhaps the most important measure requires that coordinated disaster management plans be put into place.

Because most scientists agree that global warming will lead to longer and more serious droughts, an increase in desertification, and more frequent wildfires, governments, health officials, and individual citizens must be prepared for such events. Only through preparation can the impact of global warming on human health be lessened.

Notes

1. "Climate Change 101: Science and Impacts," *Climate Change 101: Understanding and Responding to Global Climate Change*, Pew Center on Global Change, January 2009. www.pewclimate.org.
2. Brian Halweil, "The Irony of Climate: Archaeologists Suspect That a Shift in the Planet's Climate Thousands of Years Ago Gave Birth to Agriculture. Now Climate Change Could Spell the End of Farming as We Know It," Worldwatch Institiute, March-April 2005. www.worldwatch.org.
3. Halweil, "The Irony of Climate."
4. Jonatan Lassa, "Famine, Drought, Malnutrition: Defining and Fighting Hunger," *The Jakarta Post*, July 3, 2006.
5. Ulisses Confalonieri et al., "2007: Human Health," *Climate Change 2007: Impacts, Adaptation, and Vulnerability. Contribution of Working Group II to the Fourth Assessment Report of the Intergovernmental Panel on Climate Change*, eds. M.L. Parry et al. Cambridge: Cambridge University Press, 2007, p. 399.
6. Peter Mwaura, "Africans More Exposed to Drought," *Daily Nation*, January 30, 2006.
7. Confalonieri et al., "2007: Human Health," p. 399.
8. Richard Seager, "An Imminent Transition to a More Arid Climate in Southwestern North America," *Science*, vol. 316, April 5, 2007, pp. 1181–84.
9. C.B. Field et al., "2007: North America," *Climate Change 2007: Impacts, Adaptation, and Vulnerability. Contribution of Working Group II to the Fourth Assessment Report of the Intergovernmental Panel on Climate Change*, eds. M.L. Parry et al. Cambridge: Cambridge University Press, 2007, p. 623.
10. J.R. Marlon et al., "Wildfire Responses to Abrupt Climate Change in North America," *Proceedings of the National Academy of Sciences of the United States*, February 24, 2009, vol. 106, p. 2519.
11. Ken Eastwood, "Climate Change: The Smoking Gun in Australia's Firestorm," *Geographical*, April 2009, vol. 81, pp. 20–21.
12. "Damage, Pollution from Wildfires Could Surge as Western U.S. Warms," American Geophysical Union, Release No. 09-22, July 28, 2009. www.agu.org.
13. "Adaptation," *Climate Change: Health and Environmental Effects*, U.S. Environmental Protection Agency, September 8, 2009. www.epa.gov.

CHAPTER 4

Extreme Weather and Health: Hurricanes and Floods

If there is one thing that climate scientists agree on, it is that global warming will cause an increase in extreme weather, a trend that is already evident. Strong tropical cyclones (regionally called hurricanes, typhoons, or cyclones) will increase in intensity, with stronger winds, heavy rains, and devastating storm surges. Hurricane Katrina, a storm that hit the Gulf Coast of the United States in 2005, demonstrated the deadly nature of an intense hurricane. Likewise, in 2009 Cyclone Nargis slammed into the coast of Myanmar (formerly known as Burma) in Southeast Asia and killed more than 85,000 people. According to an April 2009 *New York Times* article, thousands were still missing one year later.

In addition to stronger storms, there is also the potential for extreme rainfall events, with areas receiving far more rain in a shorter period of time than in the past. The Pew Center on Global Climate Change reports that "more rain is falling in extreme events now compared to 50 years ago."[1] In addition, meteorologists are still studying the mechanisms behind El Niño, a sporadic warming in the Pacific Ocean that disrupts weather patterns across the globe. Although the connection between global warming and El Niño (as well as with its "sister," La Niña, a cooling of Pacific water temperatures often following an El Niño year) is open to debate, many climatologists agree that global warming will intensify the effects of El Niño on local weather. Some of those scientists point to El Niño in the period from 1997 to 1998 as evidence for this claim, noting that the combination of global warming and El Niño effect made 1998 the world's hottest year. Science writer Eugene Linden writes that that year produced "the strongest El Niño in 130,000 years (as evident from records encoded in ancient coral) cause[d] $100 billion damage worldwide, leaving in its wake catastrophic floods along the Yangtze in China, massive fires in Indonesian Borneo and the Brazilian Amazon, and extreme drought in Mexico and Central America."[2] Some argue that when the effects of El Niño piggyback on the effects of global warming, weather extremes can reach catastrophic proportions, causing death, injury, and disease among the populations of affected regions.

Direct Threats to Health from Extreme Weather

As the World Health Organization (WHO) points out, weather extremes—especially heavy rains, floods, and hurricanes—pose a serious risk to human health. The WHO reports approximately 600,000 deaths worldwide from weather-related catastrophes during the 1990s.[3]

Hurricanes and floods caused by excessive rains are among the most dangerous of all the health risks posed by global warming. Hurricane-force wind can lead to injury or death for anyone in its path. When a window in a house breaks during a hurricane, wind rushes in and lifts up the roof, and the house collapses upon itself, destroying belongings and injuring or killing people who have not evacuated. In addition, strong winds can lift and carry heavy objects such as construction materials or tree branches. These flying objects are like lethal weapons; exposed people in a storm could be struck by boards, nails, branches, or other debris made airborne by the wind.

Although wind is dangerous, water is more so. More people are killed by flooding and storm surges than by any other single natural disaster. Floods occur when torrential rains cause creeks and rivers to overflow their banks, or when supersaturated ground cannot absorb any more water. Sometimes, heavy rains can cause flash flooding, either by rupturing a dam or by channeling water through a narrow canyon or valley. People caught in the path of a flash flood have little warning; the lucky among them find themselves clinging to trees and awaiting rescue. The less fortunate are carried away to their deaths by drowning or traumatic injury. The Pew Center on Global Climate Change predicts that the increase in extreme rain events caused by global warming will result in more flash floods.[4]

On September 27, 2009, Tropical Storm Ketsana dumped 16.7 inches of rain in just twelve hours on Manila.

Much of the midwestern United States experienced extreme rain events in the years 1994 and 2008, resulting in flooding of epic proportions. Meteorologists called these hundred-year floods, floods that would be expected to happen only once in a century. Yet these two events happened only fifteen years apart.[5] Additionally, between 1990 and 2009, major flooding from extreme rain events has affected people across the globe. In 2003, for example, 130 million people in China were injured, killed, or displaced as a result of floods, according to researcher Ulisses Confalonieri and his colleagues, writing for the Intergovernmental Panel on Climate Change (IPCC).[6] Additionally, on September 27, 2009, Tropical Storm Ketsana dumped 16.7 inches (43 cm) of rain in just twelve hours on Manila, the capital of the Philippines. This amount is the most rain ever recorded in one day in the Philippines, and it caused serious flooding, killing more than 100 people and leaving some 280,000 people homeless, according to meteorologist Jeff Masters.[7]

In addition, many people each year are drowned or injured when they attempt to cross a flooded area in their vehicles. Few realize that moving water just 6 inches (15 cm) deep can wash away a car in minutes, plunging drivers and passengers into swirling, rapidly moving floodwaters.

Hurricanes and tropical storms also create what is known as a storm surge. A storm surge occurs when the fierce rotating winds of a tropical cyclone push water ashore. The surge combines with the incoming tide to raise water levels dramatically, as much as 15 feet to 25 feet (4.5 m to 7.6 m). Intense storms with high winds also create large waves in addition to the surge. Thus, water can rapidly accumulate on shore, destroying homes, washing away cars, and causing injury or death by drowning. The National Oceanic and Atmospheric Administration (NOAA) advises that "the greatest potential for loss of life related to a hurricane is from the storm surge."[8]

In some parts of the world, a common side effect of torrential rains from tropical storms is mud slides. In areas with steep hills that have been cleared of trees and vegetation, heavy rains can turn hillside fields into mud that then slides down the hills, destroying houses and people in its wake. In Venezuela in 1999, for example, thirty thousand people died from floods and landslides that followed storms, according to Confalonieri and his colleagues.[9]

Indirect Threats to Health from Extreme Weather

While the direct health risks of extreme weather caused by global warming may seem obvious, there are many more indirect threats. When a massive storm such as Katrina or Nargis affects a region, it creates a cascade of unsafe conditions and makes getting access to help very difficult. Indeed, such storms sometimes cause a breakdown in infrastructure. When roads are washed out or blocked by trees, medical and emergency vehicles are unable to reach the injured and dying. Rescue becomes difficult or impossible. During heavy flooding, people may be stranded on rooftops for days, awaiting rescue. For some who have managed to survive the initial onslaught of severe weather, delayed rescue ultimately costs them their lives.

Hurricane Katrina: The Worst Natural Disaster in U.S. History

On August 25, 2005, Hurricane Katrina hit Florida as a Category 1 storm and did minimal damage. Once it was over the warm waters of the Gulf of Mexico, however, Katrina strengthened dramatically to a Category 5 hurricane, a massive, swirling storm of clouds, rain, wind, and waves. Hurricane-force winds extended some 75 miles (120 km) out from the eye.

Although Katrina had weakened to a Category 3 hurricane by the time it hit the Mississippi and Louisiana coastlines on August 29, its storm surge was an impressive 24 feet to 28 feet (7.3 m to 8.5 m) in western Mississippi, 17 feet to 22 feet (5.1 m to 6.7 m) in eastern Mississippi, and 5 feet to 20 feet (1.5 m to 6 m) in Louisiana. The surge was much higher than one would expect of a Category 3 storm; Katrina's days as a Category 5 monster had set in motion the worst natural disaster in U.S. history, however, by moving huge amounts of water ashore, water that broke levees—embankments built to prevent the overflow of a river—in New Orleans and destroyed much of the Mississippi coastline.

In all, some 1,833 people lost their lives as a result of Katrina. Many, many more were seriously injured or harmed by flying debris, contaminated water, toxic spills, tornado winds, vehicular accidents during evacuation, near-drowning from floodwaters, and other hazards. Many lost their homes and suffered serious emotional and mental stress. In the years that followed, many more continued to suffer health effects from the storm.

Storm damage totaled about $81 billion. There is no estimate, however, on the long-term damage Katrina did to the health and welfare of the people of the Gulf Coast who survived her fury.

Likewise, serious storms can knock out communications among emergency personnel such as police, firefighters, medical teams, and rescue workers. Without the ability to communicate, disaster relief teams cannot answer calls for help efficiently or effectively, causing delays in services. In major floods or storms, such delays can further damage public health.

Even when the injured can be rescued and transported to medical facilities, hospitals may not have the capacity to deal with huge numbers of people injured in storms. Again, washed out or blocked roads can prevent medical personnel from getting to hospitals. In addition, some medical personnel may evacuate for their own safety when a large storm approaches, leaving hospitals understaffed.

Water Contamination and Shortages

Collapse of infrastructure is not the only indirect threat to health during floods and storms. Floodwaters, sweeping through industrial areas, can become contaminated with toxic materials such as heavy metals, chemicals, or oil slicks. People who must walk or swim through these waters to safety can endanger their health, as do rescue workers who come in contact with the toxic water. Confalonieri and coauthors predict that "increases in population density and accelerating industrial development in areas subject to natural disasters increase . . . the potential for mass human exposure to hazardous materials released during disasters."[10]

Extreme weather can result in broken gas lines and downed power lines. Broken gas lines can lead to raging fires, and, again, in industrial areas, these fires can release toxic chemicals into the atmosphere, causing injury to anyone who breathes in the fumes. In addition, downed power lines pose a potent threat to life, particularly when the lines are submerged in water. Electrocution is a risk for flood and hurricane victims and for rescue workers alike.

In the aftermath of extreme weather events, freshwater becomes a serious concern for public health. Often, drinking water resources are contaminated by sewage overflows containing fecal material, requiring people to boil their water before drinking. Power outages can mean that people do not have the means to sterilize their water and must face a choice between becoming ill from water-borne disease or from dehydration. As days pass, food reserves also become contaminated, either by flood-waters or by a lack of refrigeration due to power outages. Con-tamination of water and food supplies often leads to large-scale outbreaks of cholera, a disease caused by the bacterium *Vibro cholerae*. Symptoms of cholera include severe diarrhea and dehy-dration. According to the Mayo Clinic, cholera can quickly turn fatal without treatment.

Long-Lasting Health Effects of Extreme Weather

The indirect health effects of extreme weather can linger for months, even years, after the initial event. Standing pools of water left from flooding provide a perfect breeding ground for mosquitoes, some of which can carry malaria. In the coming de-cades, the warming climate will also mean that malarial mos-

In addition to the devastation of storm waters from Hurricane Katrina, mold caused both property damage and detrimental health effects. Chris Graythen/Getty Images.

quitoes will likely move farther north, posing a health risk for people experiencing floods in higher latitudes as well.

Likewise, after floodwaters have cleared, residual water and dampness make homes and businesses susceptible to mold infestation, particularly in a warming climate. Indeed, the Centers for Disease Control and Prevention (CDC) lists toxic mold as "the greatest risk for illness when returning to flood damaged homes, businesses, or other facilities."[11] Molds release spores into the air, and many people are highly allergic to these spores. In homes that have been flooded, large quantities of mold spores can cause breathing problems and health issues even for individuals who might not normally suffer mold allergies. Among the people at greatest risk, according to the CDC, are infants, children, and the elderly.

The Health Risks of Evacuations and Refugee Status

Another indirect threat to health from extreme weather stems, ironically, from efforts to preserve health and life. When an impending hurricane forces evacuations, large numbers of people take to the roads to avoid the storm. In the traffic jams that follow, car accidents, some serious, are common.

Furthermore, storm and flood refugees often find themselves sheltered in close quarters with many other people. Communicable diseases such as colds and influenza often affect such people. In addition, people finding themselves relocated as a result of evacuation or relocation due to storms and floods may find that they are exposed to a new host of disease-causing germs in their new surroundings. At the same time, the displaced may spread diseases among the members of their new communities.

Mental Health Suffers Because of Extreme Weather

Finally, extreme weather can affect mental health as well as physical health, according to the CDC: "From the loss of life, dis-

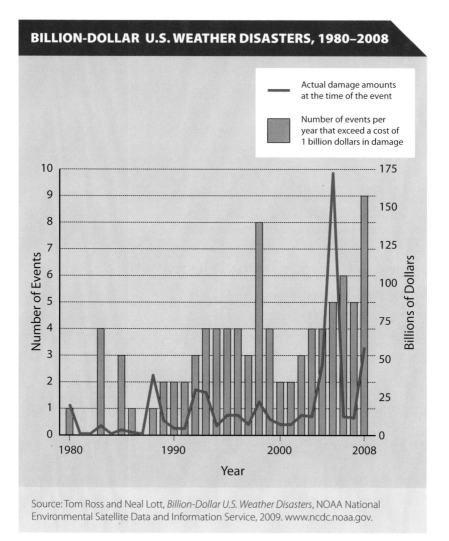

BILLION-DOLLAR U.S. WEATHER DISASTERS, 1980–2008

Actual damage amounts at the time of the event

Number of events per year that exceed a cost of 1 billion dollars in damage

Source: Tom Ross and Neal Lott, *Billion-Dollar U.S. Weather Disasters*, NOAA National Environmental Satellite Data and Information Service, 2009. www.ncdc.noaa.gov.

location, infrastructure loss, and interruption of medical care, extreme weather events such as severe hurricanes can be associated with increases in depression and post-traumatic stress disorder."[12] Survivors of major hurricanes or floods sometimes find themselves suffering from post-traumatic stress disorder, commonly known as PTSD. Many experience serious problems adjusting to their new circumstances. They may also experience depression over lost property and jobs, as well as grief for family members or others in the community who perished in the catastrophe. Long after the storms are over and the floodwaters have receded, people who have experienced such traumatic events may suffer anxiety and fear that there might be another disaster in the future and that they might have to go through a similar trauma.

The Poor Suffer the Most Health Risks

Global warming will render some communities more vulnerable to these health impacts than others. Low-lying and coastal areas will suffer from an increased number of storm surges in the coming decades. In addition, if oceans rise as some models of global warming suggest they will, storm surges will occur on top of already higher water levels, putting an ever greater percentage of the world's population at risk.

Most public health officials agree that lower-income groups living in highly populated areas or in environmentally degraded areas, common in developing nations across the globe, will suffer disproportionately from the health effects of tropical storms and flooding. The WHO predicts that "no country will be spared the consequences of climate change. But those with high levels of poverty and malnutrition, weak health infrastructure and/or political unrest will be the least able to cope."[13]

Preventing the Most Serious Health Risks

Extreme weather events—including powerful hurricanes and intense rainfall, followed by flooding—are happening in the world today. The likelihood is that these disasters will increase as the climate warms. Therefore, while it is important to work on mitigating global warming, it is also important for governments, industry, businesses, organizations, and individuals to adapt to the changing climate. The Intergovernmental Panel on Climate Change states, "Adaptation to climate change takes place through adjustments to reduce vulnerability or enhance resilience in response to observed or expected weather events."[14]

Adaptation for extreme weather events includes improving the storm-worthiness of dwellings in tropical storm–prone areas and developing disaster alert programs to make residents aware when a dangerous storm is approaching. Efficient evacuation procedures must be developed by local and regional governments to ensure a safe exit from endangered areas. In addition, improved sewage disposal and sanitation infrastructure makes it less likely that floodwater will become contaminated with human waste, and thus less likely to be a source of cholera and other water-borne illnesses. Identifying floodplains and preventing human development there will also protect human health. Ensuring that infrastructure can withstand high winds and extreme rain events will also benefit human health. Finally, well-trained rescue workers and emergency first-responders can save many lives by speedily reaching victims of hurricanes and floods.

Notes

1. "Climate Change 101: Science and Impacts," *Climate Change 101: Understanding and Responding to Global Climate Change*, Pew Center on Global Climate Change, January 2009. www.pewclimate.org.
2. Eugene Linden, *Climate, Weather and the Destruction of Civilizations*. New York: Simon and Schuster, 2006, p. 277.
3. "Climate and Health," Fact Sheet No. 266, World Health Organization, August 2007. www.who.int.
4. "Climate Change 101: Science and Impacts," Pew Center on Global Climate Change.
5. "Climate Change 101: Science and Impacts," Pew Center on Global Climate Change.
6. Ulisses Confalonieri et al., "2007: Human Health," *Climate Change 2007: Impacts, Adaptation, and Vulnerability: Contributions of Working Group II to the Fourth Assessment Report of the Intergovernmental Panel on Climate Change*, eds. M.L. Parry et al., Cambridge: Cambridge University Press, p. 398.
7. Jeff Masters, "Record Rains in Philippines from Tropical Storm Ketsana Kill at Least 106, *Weather Underground*, September 27, 2009. www.wunderground.com.
8. "Storm Surge," *Hurricane Preparedness*, National Oceanic and Atmospheric Administration. www.nhc.noaa.gov.
9. Confalonieri, "2007: Human Health," p. 398.
10. Confalonieri, "2007: Human Health," p. 399.
11. "Buildings and Facilities Damaged by Flood or Water: Health Risks," U.S. Centers for Disease Control and Prevention, April 10, 2009. www.cdc.gov.

12. "Health Effects," *Climate Change and Public Health*, U.S. Centers for Disease Control and Prevention, 2009. www.cdc.gov.

13. "Climate Change Is Bad for Your Health," World Health Organization Regional Office for the Western Pacific, April 7, 2008. www.wpro.who.int.

14. W. Neil Adger et al., "Assessment of Adaptation Practices, Options, Constraints, and Practices," *Contributions of Working Group II to the Fourth Assessment Report of the Intergovernmental Panel on Climate Change*. Cambridge: Cambridge University Press, 2007, p. 720.

CHAPTER 5

The Impact of Diminished Air Quality on Health

Human beings are remarkably resilient to diseases and health risks. Humans can live for several weeks without food, and for several days without water. No one can live for more than a few minutes without drawing a breath, however. Breathable air is the single most important factor in human survival.

Global Warming and Air Quality

For this reason, understanding the connection between global warming and air quality is crucial to the long-term survival of the human race. At the same time, the connection is highly complex: Air pollution is not only one of the *effects* of global warming, it is also one of the *causes*. As the Nobel Prize–winning organization Physicians for Social Responsibility points out, "The burning of coal, oil, and natural gas produces not only greenhouse gases, but also a range of harmful air pollutants, including ozone, airborne particulates, sulfur dioxide, and nitrogen oxide."[1] Thus, burning carbon-based products increases global warming through the release of carbon dioxide and other greenhouse gases. At the same time, global warming may harm air quality and human health in at least five major ways:

- Global warming speeds ozone formation, which in turn contributes to further warming and causes serious health problems

- Global warming leads to more smog and particulate matter emissions, which are also known health risks
- Global warming leads to heat waves, further accelerating ozone formation
- Global warming may lead to increased wildfires that introduce smoke, soot, ash, and other fine particulates into the air
- Global warming may lead to more aero-allergens such as pollens and molds

Ozone: Friend and Foe

Any discussion of global warming and air quality must first look at the role ozone plays in human health and disease, starting with an explanation of what ozone is. For human survival, the most important component of air is oxygen; air is a gas that consists of two atoms of oxygen (O_2). The gas known as ozone (O_3) consists of three atoms of oxygen. According to the National Aeronautics and Space Administration (NASA), stratospheric ozone protects life on Earth by shielding the planet's surface from the ultraviolet (UV) rays of the sun. By so doing, states the U.S. Environmental Protection Agency (EPA), ozone reduces "human exposure to harmful UV radiation that causes skin cancer and cataracts."[2] Nearly 90 percent of the total ozone found in the atmosphere sits in the stratosphere, about 5 miles to 30 miles (8 km to 48 km) above the earth's surface, where it exists in a kind of balance: Sunlight creates ozone, and certain chemical reactions (some human-made) destroy it. Stratospheric ozone is absolutely essential for life on Earth, and holes in the ozone layers are of great concern to scientists, government officials, and citizens.

Ozone also exists in the troposphere, the layer of atmosphere closest to the earth's surface. This ozone damages human health and is a primary component of smog and air pollution. According to the world's oldest scientific academy, the Royal Society, "Ozone is formed when sunlight reacts with pollutants and naturally occurring chemicals in the air. These chemicals come from such sources as vehicle exhaust fumes and forest fires."[3] Ozone production is particularly high when the weather is hot and sunny and the air stagnant. In the United States on such days, the EPA declares "ozone action days." This declaration provides instructions to citizens as to how they can help reduce ozone pollution by, for example, driving their cars less. An ozone action day alert also provides information about how individuals should protect their own health, particularly the health of children and anyone with chronic lung disorders such as asthma or chronic obstructive pulmonary disorder. These conditions are increasingly likely in some parts of the world as a result of global warming.

Ozone Is a Serious Threat to Health

Breathing high concentrations of ozone is a serious threat to health. NASA states, "Shortness of breath, dry cough or pain when taking a deep breath, tightness of the chest, wheezing, and sometimes even nausea are common responses to ozone."[4] When ozone enters the human throat and lungs, it damages the lining of these airways, causing inflammation.

The EPA has ruled that exposure to ozone levels of over 80 parts per billion for eight hours or longer poses serious health risks, including throat and lung irritation, asthma, and emphysema. (Parts per billion is a common measurement of the concentration of pollution in the air or water; one way to think of it is as one drop of ink in a tank that holds one billion drops of water.) The Puget Sound Clean Air Agency notes that "ozone may damage lung tissue even in healthy people. It makes our eyes itch, burn and water. Even healthy people can be affected if they exercise outdoors."[5] Indeed, the National Institute of Environmental Health Sciences (NIEHS) conducted tests that revealed reduced lung capacity in people exercising for even short periods of time when ozone levels are at 80 parts per billion.

While the short-term damage incurred by ozone may be reversible, NASA reports:

Exposure to ozone levels we commonly encounter in many of our own communities permanently scars the lungs of experimental animals, causing long-term impairment of lung capacity, or the volume of air that can be expelled from fully inflated lungs. Ozone may have similar effects on human lungs. Studies in animals suggest that ozone may reduce the human immune system's ability to fight bacterial infections in the respiratory system.[6]

Medical researchers and doctors are particularly concerned over the long-term effects of ozone pollution on the lungs of children,

Global Warming May Be Spurring Allergy and Asthma

There's growing scientific evidence that global climate change is linked to the dramatic rise in allergies and asthma in the Western world. Studies have found that a higher level of carbon dioxide turbocharges the growth of plants whose pollen triggers allergies. In 2001 Lewis Ziska planted ragweed—the main cause of hay fever in the fall—at urban, suburban, and rural sites near Baltimore. The plots had the same seeds and soil and were watered in the same way. Yet the downtown plants soon exploded in size, flowering earlier and producing five times the pollen of rural plants. The city pollen was a lot more toxic, too. The likely cause? The city plants experienced warmer temperatures and 20% more carbon dioxide, the effect of more cars and pollution.

"We can see the changes now, and they already have implications for public health," says Dr. Ziska, a plant physiologist at the U.S. Department of Agriculture. Allergies and asthma are closely linked; more than 70% of asthma sufferers also have allergies.

SOURCE: Gautam Naik, "Global Warming May Be Spurring Allergy, Asthma: Dr. Ziska's Ragweed Loves Carbon Dioxide; Toxic Pollen in Cities?" *Wall Street Journal*, May 10, 2007, p. A1.

who not only spend more time outdoors but also breathe in more ozone per pound of body weight than do adults, according to NASA. All agree that ozone inhalation worsens asthma and cardiopulmonary diseases, so people suffering from these ailments are at special risk on the hot days of summer, and at a growing risk as the number of hot days of summer increase across the globe.

Smog and Air Quality

Smog is a portmanteau word, that is, one created by combining two words, in this case "smoke" and "fog." Smog first came into the English language about 1905. Little wonder that the word was coined during the very early years of the twentieth century: From the nineteenth century onward, increasing industrialization in major cities led to the widespread burning of coal and gasoline. The thick, smoky haze belching out of steel factory chimneys often covered such cities as Pittsburgh, Pennsylvania, and Newcastle, England. Later, the introduction of gas-burning automobiles contributed fumes and pollution to the smoggy air. During the summer especially, these emissions cook under the hot sun and form thick blankets of smog, containing high concentrations of ozone and other pollutants. As developing countries become increasingly urbanized and industrial and join the developed countries of the world in the burning of fossil fuels and the use of chemicals, air quality worldwide suffers from both smog and particulate pollution. The National Academy of Sciences asserts, "Human activities produce or enhance the release of a wide range of airborne substances that affect air quality; and poor air quality has long been recognized as an undesirable side effect of urban population concentrations and intensive industrial and agricultural activities."[7]

Global warming increases the climatic conditions that make smog more prevalent. Atmospheric inversions, for example—weather events in which the air temperature increases with altitude rather than decreases—trap smog close to the earth. Because the air closest to the ground is cooler and heavier in an

Hotter summers could worsen already unhealthful smog conditions in cities such as Linfen in China's Shanxi province, one of the most polluted cities in the world. Peter Parks/AFP/Getty Images.

inversion than the very hot air above, it does not rise and thus does not create breezes that would disperse the smog. Therefore, hot, dry summers, with frequent atmospheric inversions, create air stagnation in many urban areas such as Los Angeles, California, and Mumbai, India, with all the health threats and risks connected to high ozone levels.

Particulate Matter: Sources and Spread

Smog may also contain particulate matter, though some forms of particulate matter can circulate in rural areas as well as urban centers, minus smog. Particulate matter is simply any small or fine matter that floats in the air. Mostly, these particles are invisible. Although unseen, they nonetheless are the source of the most serious health risks connected with diminished air quality.

Particulate matter comes from a variety of sources. Particles may come from smoke, dirt, and dust created by factories, dirt roads, or farming. Often, they are created when rocks are crushed or the soil is disturbed; the particles are then blown by the wind. Some very fine particles are emitted from metal processing and smelting, fires, or automobile fumes. These particles can be composed of toxic compounds or heavy metals, such as mercury. Some particulate matter is actually liquid in the form of tiny droplets, sometimes including lung-damaging chemicals, produced by industrial processes. In addition, a notable source of all types of airborne particulate matter is power plant emissions. As the planet warms, there will be greater demands on power plants to produce electricity for refrigeration and air conditioning, demands that can result in an even greater amount of particulate-laden emissions from power plants. In addition, a 2009 British study led by environmental chemist Alistair B.A. Boxall of the University of York demonstrates many ways that humans can be indirectly exposed to pathogens and chemicals from agriculture. Boxall and colleagues write, "Humans may be exposed to agriculturally derived chemicals and pathogens in the environment (i.e., air, soil, water, sediment) by a number of routes. . . . Exposure may . . . occur via the inhalation of particulates."[8]

The Health Effects of Smog and Particulate Pollution

In 2008, the EPA released a study demonstrating that smog and particulate pollution is likely to grow worse with global warming. In addition to increased power plant emissions, drought-stricken farmland will kick up more dust, much of it laden with agricultural chemicals. As Boxall and his colleagues conclude, "Overall, climate change is likely to increase human exposure to agricultural contaminants."[9]

Global warming is also expected to increase the number of wildfires. These fires shoot soot and ash into the air, causing a concentration of particulate matter and a degradation of air quality. In addition, when fires burn uncontrolled through housing developments or industrial settings, the toxic chemicals in building materials or factories also become part of the particulate soup.

Each year, 200,000 to 570,000 people die from exposure to air pollution.

The EPA prediction therefore suggests that the health problems associated with smog and particulate pollution may also increase. As the Physicians for Social Responsibility argue, "Exposure to air pollution can aggravate chronic respiratory and cardiovascular disease, damage lung tissue, lead to premature death, and may even contribute to cancer. Global warming may exacerbate these problems."[10]

In May 2008, California Institute of Technology researchers Shinichi Enami, M.R. Hoffmann, and A.J. Colussi released a study that demonstrated the mechanism through which airborne particulates damage lung tissue. Their research suggests that airborne particulates damage the lungs' ability to defend against ozone damage. Thus, the combination of ozone and particulate pollution is doubly damaging to lung tissue. Colussi, quoted in the May 15, 2008, issue of *Science Daily*, noted, "Epidemiologists had consistently found significant increases in emergency-room admissions and cardiorespiratory deaths during episodes of high levels of both atmospheric ozone and particulates in several American and European cities."[11] He further surmised that the two pollutants, working together, did more harm than either pollutant working separately.

People exposed to high levels of particulate matter can suffer from cardiac arrhythmia (an irregular beating of the heart), asthma, and cardiovascular disease. Individuals who already suffer from chronic bronchitis or emphysema are likely to have their conditions aggravated by smog and particulate pollution. Additionally, the damage to the lining of the lungs from the combined effects of ozone and particulate matter renders the body more vulnerable to attack from communicable respiratory diseases such as pneumonia and influenza. NASA reports that particulate matter is the form of air pollution "most prominently linked to premature death."[12] The American Lung Association estimates that power plant emissions alone trigger some 366,000 asthma attacks a year, and that 200,000 to 570,000 people die each year from exposure to air pollution.[13]

Aero-Allergens and Health

Aero-allergens are simply any airborne substances that create an allergic response in humans. Examples include pollen, mold, spores, or fungi. Global warming may increase the concentration, geographic range, and incidence of aero-allergens for several reasons. First, the increase in temperatures and carbon dioxide in the atmosphere caused by global warming are likely to lead to more pollen-producing plants. In addition, these plants will have a longer growing season, extending the period during which they spread their pollen. Hot windy weather also spreads plant matter far afield, leading to widespread allergic reactions.

Areas not experiencing dry weather conducive to the spread of plant pollens will not escape the potential of airborne allergens, however. Damp, humid, and warm conditions will foster the growth of molds, both indoors and out, as well as fungi. While most molds are harmless, some of them produce mycotoxins, chemicals that can be dangerous to health. In addition, airborne mold spores can cause serious allergic responses in children and adults. According to the Michigan Department of Community Health, "the most common health problems due to mold exposure are runny nose, sinus congestion, eye irritation, cough and congestion, sore throat, sneezing, upper respiratory infections, headaches, worsening asthma, and fatigue."[14]

Some areas in the Midwest and Great Lakes regions of the United States suffered from serious black mold infestations in homes and businesses during the 2000s, as a result of ice dams that built up in eaves, lifting up roof shingles. This, in turn, allowed melting snow and rain water to leak into attics and walls. Because houses in this region of the country tend to be well-insulated, and there was little air circulation, dangerous levels of mold invaded the homes. Mold spores were subsequently released into the air of the houses or businesses and sickened many residents. Many homes had to be cleaned by hazardous materials specialists; some had to be completely gutted or even destroyed to eliminate the mold. Because global warming models suggest that this area of the country will have heavier winter precipitation, the danger of mold infestation continues to pose a health risk.

Like molds, fungi thrive in warm, moist environments. These environments will be more common because of global warming and will encourage the spread of potentially dangerous fungi into new habitats. One example is *Cryptococcus gattii*, a microscopic tropical fungus that has newly made an appearance in British Columbia and the American Pacific Northwest. According to the U.S. Centers for Disease Control and Prevention and

AIR POLLUTION AND HEALTH

Air Quality Index	Protect Your Health
Good (0–50)	No health impacts are expected when the air quality is in this range.
Moderate (51–100)	Unusually sensitive people should consider limiting prolonged outdoor exertion.
Unhealthy for Sensitive Groups (101–150)	The following groups should limit prolonged outdoor exertion: • People with lung disease, such as asthma • Children and older adults • People who are active outdoors
Unhealthy (151–200)	The following groups should avoid prolonged outdoor exertion: • People with lung disease, such as asthma • Children and older adults • People who are active outdoors Everyone else should limit prolonged outdoor exertion.
Very Unhealthy (201–300)	The following groups should avoid all outdoor exertion: • People with lung disease, such as asthma • Children and older adults • People who are active outdoors Everyone else should limit outdoor exertion.

Source: United States Environmental Protection Agency, *Ozone and Your Health*, February 2009.

the BC [British Columbia] Centre for Disease Control, people can develop cryptococcosis, a life-threatening infection of the lungs and, more rarely, the central nervous system from inhaling the airborne spores of the fungus. People with healthy immune systems and ones with compromised immune systems (for example, individuals who suffer from HIV infection) can contract the illnesses caused by the fungus. Symptoms often include prolonged cough, severe headache, fever, night sweats, and weight loss. Skin lesions are also common among the infected. Because it often takes two months or more for symptoms to be evident, diagnosis of the disease can be difficult, though patients can be successfully treated with antifungal drugs.

Life's Breath: Air Quality in a Warming World

Because climate change cannot be easily or quickly halted, many of the problems of air quality will continue to plague the human and animal populations of the earth. Ozone formation, for example, is likely to continue so long as emissions remain high and temperatures climb. Likewise, airborne allergens will continue to pose threats to people who have allergies because of longer growing seasons and wider dispersal.

Nevertheless, there are many ways that the quality of indoor and outdoor air can be improved, steps that will go a long way toward protecting the lungs of young children especially. First, expanding the system of alerting populations when the levels of ozone exceed 80 parts per billion will allow parents and schools to keep children indoors on those days. Media such as television and radio can aid in this effort, in much the same way that they announce other weather-related events, such as winter weather advisories and severe thunderstorm warnings. Second, public health officials, schools, local governments, and other institutions can mount education efforts to inform the public of the dangers of ozone and smog exposure, encouraging people to pay attention to ozone action day alerts.

Governments can also play a part in ensuring that citizens have clean air to breathe, in spite of global warming. Regulations on emissions from automobiles, power plants, and factories will help improve air quality by reducing not only ozone, but also particulate matter. Many climate change experts and policy makers assert that the governments of developed nations must find ways to help developing nations establish cleaner factories and power plants.

This notion of government regulation, however, is a source of controversy throughout the world. In developed nations, citizens have come to expect the comforts of life that cars, air conditioning, central heating, and material goods provide. Giving up material comforts in exchange for the promise of cleaner air—something that the average person can neither observe nor measure—can be difficult. In addition, in developed nations, industries are already subject to numerous regulations related to emissions and waste products. Many business owners chafe under current regulations and protest that further regulations will make their businesses unprofitable.

Developing nations want to establish strong manufacturing bases and enter the global economy as full partners. To do so, these nations often build factories and power plants that do not include devices to safeguard the air, because these devices add great expense to manufacturing processes. In addition, like their counterparts in the developed world, citizens of developing countries want cars and goods to increase the comfort of their own lives. As more and more of the world's population gains access to these items, the stress on air quality resulting from the processes that produce such goods dramatically increases. Finally, developing nations do not want the powerful, developed nations of the world to impose rules and regulations on them.

Mitigating Harmful Effects

While medical researchers are working diligently to find treatments and cures for diseases caused by airborne allergens, including pollens, molds, and fungi, other scientists are researching ways to reduce air pollution itself. Individuals need to consider how they can help stop pollution through their actions, as they also pay close attention to their own health and to the health of their family members. People should be alert to the symptoms of diseases caused or made worse by poor air quality and should work with their doctors to find the best treatment possible, especially for cases of childhood asthma, a life-threatening disease.

Education, planning, regulation, and research will do much to mitigate the harmful effects of diminished air quality created by global warming. In addition, the reduction of harmful greenhouse gases and emissions will not only improve air quality, it will also slow global warming itself.

Notes

1. "Air Quality," Physicians for Social Responsibility, 2009. www.psr.org.
2. "Ozone and Your Patients' Health: Training for Health Care Providers," U.S. Environmental Protection Agency, October 7, 2007. www.epa.gov.
3. "Ozone Controls Failing to Protect Human Health and the Environment," The Royal Society, October 6, 2008. http://royalsociety.org.
4. "The Ozone We Breathe: Ozone's Effects on Human Health," *Earth Observatory*, National Aeronautics and Space Administration, October 9, 2009. http://earthobservatory.nasa.gov.
5. "What Is Smog?" Puget Sound Clean Air Agency, 2009. www.pscleanair.org.
6. "The Ozone We Breathe," *Earth Observatory*.
7. "Global Sources of Local Pollution: An Assessment of Long-Range Transport of Key Air Pollutants to and from the United States," National Research Council of the National Academies, National Academies Press, 2009, p. 10.
8. Alistair B.A. Boxall et al., "Impacts of Climate Change on Indirect Human Exposure to Pathogens and Chemicals from Agriculture," *Environmental Health Perspectives*, vol. 117, April 2009, pp. 508–15.
9. Boxall et al., "Impacts of Climate Change on Indirect Human Exposure to Pathogens and Chemicals from Agriculture," p. 508.
10. "The Medical and Public Health Impacts of Global Warming: A Fact Sheet from the Physicians for Social Responsibility," Physicians for Social Responsibility, 2009. www.psr.org/resources/the-medical-and-public-health-impacts-of-global-warming.pdf.
11. "Chemistry of Airborne Particulate: Lung Interactions Revealed," *Science Daily*, May 15, 2008. www.sciencedaily.com.
12. "The Ozone We Breathe," *Earth Observatory*.
13. "Key Facts About Air Pollution," American Lung Association, 2004. www.lungusa.org.
14. "Mold: Information for the Public," Michigan Department of Community Health, June 9, 2006. www.michigan.gov.

CHAPTER **6**

Global Warming and Infectious Disease

One of the most commonly circulated scientific predictions concerning the impact of global warming is that the incidence of both vector-borne and zoonotic diseases will increase as the climate heats up. A vector is an agent that carries an infection from one human or animal host to another human or animal host. For example, when a particular species of mosquito bites someone with dengue fever, it carries the disease with it when it bites the next person, who then becomes infected. Lyme disease, malaria, and Rocky Mountain spotted fever are three additional examples of vector-borne diseases. These diseases are also known as arboviruses, because they are spread for the most part by arthropods, invertebrates that have segmented bodies and external skeletons, such as spiders, mosquitoes, and ticks.

A zoonotic disease, on the other hand, is one that transmits from vertebrate animals to humans, sometimes directly, and sometimes through means of a vector. For example, rabies can be transmitted to humans directly from an infected animal such as a bat or fox. West Nile disease is an example of a vector-borne zoonotic disease: A mosquito that bites a bird infected with the virus can then infect a human being with the same virus, simply through a bite.

Vector-Borne and Zoonotic Illnesses

Many scientists argue that global warming will increase vector-borne and zoonotic illnesses through a number of different

Dengue Fever on the Rise

Around the world, the incidence of dengue fever has risen thirty-fold in the last 50 years, with increases across all key indicators: the number of cases, the frequency of epidemics, the severity of the disease, and the geographic range over which outbreaks occur. Each year the virus is responsible for 50 million to 100 million infections, a half-million hospitalizations, and 22,000 deaths, in more than 100 countries. Many experts believe that dengue is now the most worrisome arthropod-borne virus, or arbovirus, in the world. . . . And now it's making its way into the United States.

For most Americans, dengue remains an under-the-radar threat. But as the virus creeps northward, we need to be much more alert. . . . Dengue's proliferation can be attributed to several interconnected factors: rising temperatures and altered rainfall patterns due to climate change, population booms in impoverished urban areas with inadequate municipal services, increased international travel and trade, compromised or dismantled mosquito-reduction programs, and the glut of man-made containers (especially those made of plastic or rubber) that serve as ideal mosquito-breeding sites. . . .

Scientists project that the incidence, range, and severity of infections will continue to increase over the coming decades. As temperatures rise, the habitat suitable for vector mosquitoes expands, as does the length of disease transmission seasons in temperate zones. Moreover, when it's hotter outside, the dengue virus replicates more rapidly in the mosquito. This increases the number of days on which it can distribute the disease during its three- or four-week life span. Higher temperatures also cause the mosquito to feed more vigorously. All these factors increase its capacity to disperse the virus.

SOURCE: Kim Larsen, "The New Diseases on Our Doorstep," *OnEarth*, Fall 2009. www.onearth.org.

mechanisms. First, higher temperatures may shorten the time needed for the pathogens to develop in vectors. When a mosquito bites someone with malaria, for example, it takes a certain amount of time for the malaria-causing parasites to develop. Before this happens, the mosquito can bite another human without consequences for the human. But once the malarial parasites are well established in a mosquito, the mosquito can pass the infection. Warmer temperatures may shorten the time it takes for the disease to be established in the vector. This, in turn, leads to a longer period in which the vector can transmit the disease to humans. Theoretically, this could increase the number of humans infected.

A second concern is that the changing climate may allow vectors and animal hosts to expand their ranges. Animals and insects that could previously survive only in the lower latitudes because of their need for warm temperatures may expand their ranges northward, into the higher latitudes, as temperatures increase in these areas. For example, according to Canadian medical researchers Amy Greer and her colleagues, Lyme disease is not currently common in Canada. She adds, however, "Temper-

A girl lies beneath a mosquito net recovering from dengue fever in Nicaragua. As climate shifts, mosquitoes migrate and spread such diseases to new territories. Jorge S. Cabrera A./ LatinContent/Getty Images.

ature determines the northernmost extent of tick populations. Mathematical models suggest that tick abundance may greatly increase in southern Canada, with a northern expansion of about 200km per year by the year 2020."[1] Because ticks are vectors for Lyme disease, the likelihood, according to Greer and the other researchers, is that Lyme disease will become much more common throughout Canada. In addition, these researchers also believe that the expanded tick range will lead to a greater incidence of Lyme disease in Europe. According to epidemiologist Paul R. Epstein, ticks are moving north, infesting Sweden. In addition, he states, "Mosquitoes are appearing in mountainous regions where plant communities and freezing levels have shifted upward and glaciers are rapidly retreating." Epstein further notes that "changes in mountain ecosystems are consistent with projections, and the biological and physical observations are consistent with one another."[2]

In the United States there are currently more than 210 million cases of food-borne and water-borne diseases annually, with 900,000 of them requiring hospitalization and 6,000 leading to death.

Likewise, warmer temperatures may lead to a greater abundance of vectors. Milder winters and warmer summers could mean longer life spans and more prolific reproduction of insects and arthropods. In addition, excess rainfall and flooding also provide ample breeding grounds and extensive habitats for mosquitoes and other disease-carrying arthropods.

Increasing temperatures may also increase the number of so-called reservoir animals, such as rats. These animals are hosts for arthropods carrying diseases that can be passed to humans. For example, fleas residing on rats carry bubonic plague. Most people believe that bubonic plague was a disease limited to the Middle Ages; however, plague continues to exist throughout the world in the twenty-first century. An increase in the number of rats may increase the likelihood of plague in humans and make it much more widespread than it is currently.

An Increase in Water-Borne and Food-Borne Diseases

In addition to zoonotic and vector-borne diseases, global warming is likely to increase both water-borne and food-borne diseases. According to the Centers for Disease Control and Prevention (CDC), in the United States there are currently more than 210 million cases of food-borne and water-borne diseases annually, with 900,000 of them requiring hospitalization and 6,000 leading to death.[3] Bacteria, viruses, or parasites that thrive in humid, warm places cause most of these diseases.

Salmonella is one such bacterium. In warm, humid places, it proliferates and can make its way into food sources in several ways. First, eggs or meat can acquire the bacteria through food processing plants or in farmyards. If meat or eggs are cooked properly, the bacteria are killed and do not pose a threat. The increased incidence of salmonella in the food chain increases the chance that it will make its way into the human digestive tract because of undercooked food or poorly handled food, however. Second, when cooked foods are not cooled quickly enough, if any bacteria have survived the cooking process, they quickly multiply and sicken anyone who eats the food they contaminate. In food that is cooled properly, however, bacterial growth is dramatically slowed and remains insufficient to cause harm. Finally, if food preparation workers are suffering from a salmonella infection, they can taint the food they are preparing. Again, if hot food is kept hot and cold food is kept cold, it is less likely that contamination will lead to illness. Warmer temperatures will make it more difficult to cool foods properly, however, and make the incidence of salmonella in food sources more likely.

Another example of bacteria-borne illness is Legionnaires' disease, caused by bacteria that grow in places such as air con-

MALARIA LIFE CYCLE

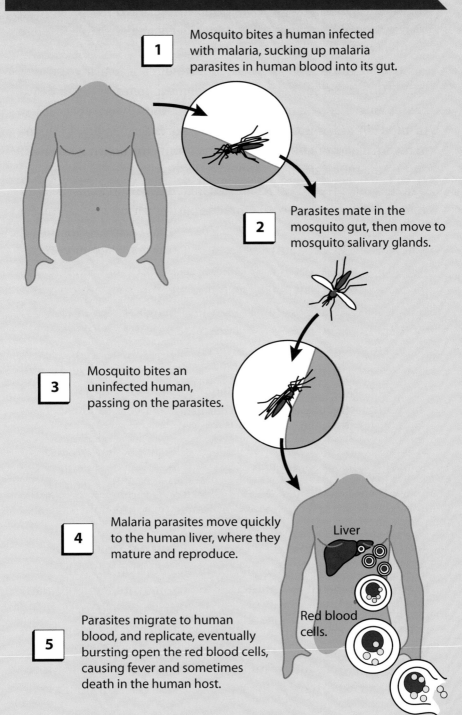

1 Mosquito bites a human infected with malaria, sucking up malaria parasites in human blood into its gut.

2 Parasites mate in the mosquito gut, then move to mosquito salivary glands.

3 Mosquito bites an uninfected human, passing on the parasites.

4 Malaria parasites move quickly to the human liver, where they mature and reproduce.

Liver

Red blood cells.

5 Parasites migrate to human blood, and replicate, eventually bursting open the red blood cells, causing fever and sometimes death in the human host.

Source: Compiled by the author, based on information from www.malaria.org.

ditioning systems and even in water fountains. As the climate warms, more people may be exposed to Legionnaires' disease because of an increased use of air conditioning.

Global warming results in additional mechanisms through which illnesses can be spread through water or food. When heavy rains flood water systems, sewage (often entirely unprocessed, or raw) contaminates drinking water, spreading bacteria and organisms that can cause cholera or cryptosporidium, a parasitic disease of the intestines. Greer and her colleagues state, "Globally, the water-borne enteric [intestinal] disease most likely to increase in the face of global climate change is cholera, a diarrheal disease with a high case-fatality rate . . . which remains an important cause of death in the developing world."[4] These bacteria and organisms survive better and longer in warmer temperatures, so global warming may make the infections they cause more common in larger sections of the world. Brazilian researcher Ulisses Confalonieri and fellow researchers also note that "contact between food and pest species, especially flies, rodents, and cockroaches is largely driven by temperature. . . . In temperate countries, warmer weather and milder winters are likely to increase the abundance of flies and other pests."[5] Because these pests carry disease, it is likely that they will be a source of food-borne illnesses.

While the examples above have focused on places where the world is becoming warmer and wetter, other places will become hotter and drier. Those areas suffering from drought will also have disease concerns related to climate change. For example, according to Confalonieri and his colleagues, meningococcal meningitis, a serious infection of the blood that is highly infectious and often causes death, can "be strongly linked to climatic and environmental factors, particularly drought." The arid, dusty conditions associated with drought appear to aid in the spread of meningitis. He also asserts that during periods of drought, mosquito populations diminish, and thus the spread of malaria is reduced. During droughts, then, people lose their immunity to malaria. Confalonieri and his colleagues write, "When the drought breaks, there is a much larger proportion of susceptible hosts to become infected, thus potentially increasing transmission."[6]

Indigenous peoples of the Arctic regions also are at risk for food-borne and water-borne illnesses as a result of global warming. Indeed, Daniel J. Weiss, senior fellow at the American Progress Foundation, and his co-writer Robin Pam call the increased incidence of water-borne and food-borne illnesses in the Arctic regions "inevitable." As the temperatures rise, the traditional ways of preparing food become more dangerous. In the Arctic, the Inuit traditionally eat many of their foods raw; animals and fish that carry bacteria such as salmonella will cause illness when eaten raw or when not stored at cold enough temperatures. In addition, food is often kept for a long time, and the food becomes either accidentally or intentionally putrefied. This includes fermented and dried food as well. In addition, according to Weiss and Pam, "increases in ocean temperatures have been linked to outbreaks of gastroenteritis . . . which may have been acquired through consumption of contaminated seafood."[7]

An Increase in Fungal Diseases

Fungal diseases are likely to increase as a result of global warming. *Cryptococcus gattii*, for example, is a tropical fungus that causes serious infections in both humans and animals. Although well known in areas such as Australia and Africa, the fungus was unknown in North America until 2001, when British Columbia veterinarians first identified it there. Researchers at the University of British Columbia were able to determine that North Americans had been contracting the disease since at least 1999, but because the fungus had never previously been seen outside the tropics, the disease went undiagnosed for several years. According to Sarah Kidd of the British Columbia Cryptococcal Working Group, the fungus has been documented "on trees, in soil, in the air, and in water at many different areas of Vancouver Island" as well as in air samples from other parts of British

Columbia.[8] The fungus appeared for the first time in the United States in 2007 in the state of Washington. Since then it has been identified in Oregon as well. Johns Hopkins School of Medicine researcher Kausik Datta and colleagues argue,

> Long-term climate changes, such as the significantly elevated global temperature in the last 100 years, influence patterns of disease among plants and animals and create niche microclimates habitable by emerging pathogens. *C. gattii* may have exploited such a hitherto unrecognized but clement [favorable] environment in the Pacific Northwest to provide a wider exposure and risk of infection to human and animal populations.[9]

In other words, as temperatures in North America climb, regions previously too cold for such fungi as *Cryptococcus gattii* will become more conducive to fungal infestations. Consequently, residents of these regions will be more frequently exposed to, and suffer infections from, fungi such as this.

Global Warming and Forced Migration

Global warming poses yet another threat to human health and welfare: Environmental conditions may force people to leave their homes. For example, if an area is flooded, many residents must find new places to live, either in shelters or in temporary housing. Likewise, people who are the victims of long-term drought often are forced into refugee status. Human migration, caused by environmental factors such as drought or flooding, will lead to the intermingling of populations, and new diseases may be introduced in areas where people have not yet built immunity, according to Greer et al. Indeed, these researchers suggest that "forced migration may ultimately be a more important driver of changes in infectious disease epidemiology"[10] than many of the other effects being discussed by scientists.

In addition, people crowded together in refugee camps or shelters are more likely to contract food-borne and water-borne illnesses. Such places rarely have adequate refrigeration or cooking facilities, and cleanliness in food preparation may be an impossibility. Often, water supplies for refugees are limited or tainted.

Furthermore, when people live in close quarters, a greater likelihood exists that communicable diseases such as colds, influenza, and pneumonia will run rampant. Although some scientists predict that warmer, shorter winters may reduce the incidence of influenza worldwide, the reduction of air quality may increase diseases such as bronchitis and pneumonia. Such communicable diseases are likely to pose a greater threat to those individuals who find themselves forced to migrate or flee from environmental dangers than to the world's population at large. Diseases such as influenza, colds, and pneumonia are caused by inhaling airborne viruses or by touching surfaces that an infected person has touched. Again, the crowded conditions of refugee shelters are prime environments for such diseases to be passed from person to person.

The Debate over Global Warming and Infectious Diseases

Not all scientists agree, however, with the notion that with climate change comes more exposure to infectious diseases. Notably, U.S. Geological Survey researcher Kevin D. Lafferty, pointing out that "the link between climate change and infectious disease is complex," argues that there are numerous reasons climate change might *not* lead to an increase in diseases. His first argument is that "most species, including infectious diseases, have upper and lower limits to their temperature tolerance. This means that changes in climate should often lead to shifts, not expansions, in habitat suitability." In other words, although a habitat might move northward, it will not be a larger habitat, as it will shrink from the south. He concludes,

It seems plausible that the geographic distribution of some infectious diseases may actually experience a net decline with climate change. While this is the reverse of the conventional wisdom, it is consistent with the increasingly accepted view that climate change will reduce biodiversity.[11]

University of California-Berkeley animal ecologist Richard S. Ostfeld suggests that other factors may be more important than climate in predicting the spread of infectious diseases. He notes that interventions such as using insecticides and destroying vector breeding grounds have already proved successful in limiting the range of dengue fever and malaria; he also notes, however, that interventions are more successful in developed rather than developing countries, due to the costs such interventions incur.[12]

Oxford University professor of parasite ecology Sarah E. Randolph also argues against blaming an increase in infectious diseases on climate change. She asserts that the complex interactions of diseases, people, and the environment make attributing disease to any one factor, such as climate change, "ill-founded." Furthermore, she states bluntly, "There is no single infectious disease whose increased incidence over recent decades can be reliably attributed to climate change."[13]

Regardless of the debate over the causes and extent of increasing rates of diseases such as dengue fever, malaria, water-borne and food-borne illnesses, and fungal diseases, public health officials around the globe are working to find ways to protect human health. In the coming years, new vaccines and drugs may be developed to help people who have become infected. In addition, special attention will be given to eliminating mosquito breeding grounds. Public water systems will be subject to close scrutiny so that they continue to provide safe water. Food preparation must be carefully supervised as well. Through education and action, the world's population can be better positioned to deal with evolving challenges to human health, whatever the cause.

Notes

1   Amy Greer, Victoria Ng, and David Fisman, "Climate Change and Infectious Disease in North America: The Road Ahead," *Canadian Medical Association Journal.* March 11, 2008, p. 717.

2. Paul R. Epstein, "Climate Change and Infectious Disease: Stormy Weather Ahead?" *Epidemiology*, vol. 14, July 2002, pp. 373–75.

3. "Health Effects," *Climate Change and Public Health*, U.S. Centers for Disease Control and Prevention, 2009. www.cdc.gov.

4. Greer et al., "Climate Change and Infectious Disease in North America," p. 719.

5. Ulisses Confalonieri et al., "2007: Human Health," *Climate Change 2007: Impacts, Adaptations, and Vulnerability. Contribution of Working Group II to the Fourth Assessment Report of the Intergovernmental Panel on Climate Change*, eds. M.L. Parry et al. Cambridge: Cambridge University Press, 2007, p. 400.

6. Confalonieri et al., "2007: Human Health," p. 400.

7. Daniel J. Weiss and Robin Pam, "The Human Side of Global Warming," Center for American Progress, April 10, 2008, p. 720. www.americanprogress.org.

8. Sarah Kidd, "*Cryptococcus gattii* in BC," *Cryptococcus Gattii: Research at the University of British Columbia*, May 13, 2009. www.cryptococcusgattii.ca.

9. Kausik Datta, Karen H. Bartlett, and Kieran A. Marr, "*Cryptococcus gattii:* Emergence in Western North America: Exploitation of a Novel Ecological Niche," *Interdisciplinary Perspectives on Infectious Diseases*, vol. 2009, January 15, 2009. www.hindawi.com.

10. Greer et al., "Climate Change and Infectious Disease in North America," p. 719.

11. Kevin D. Lafferty, "The Ecology of Climate Change and Infectious Diseases," *Ecology*, vol. 90, April 2009, pp. 888–900.

12. Richard S. Ostfeld, "Climate Change and the Distribution and Intensity of Infectious Diseases," *Ecology*, vol. 90, April 2009, pp. 903–05.

13. Sarah E. Randolph, "Perspectives on Climate Change Impacts on Infectious Diseases," *Ecology*, vol. 90, April 2009, pp. 927–30.

CHAPTER 7

Food and Water: Access and Safety

After air, food and water are the two most important necessities for human life and health. People can live for two or three days without water, and for several weeks without food, but long-term survival without them is impossible. Chronic dehydration and malnutrition lead to a host of additional health problems. Thus, two key areas to consider when exploring the connections among global warming, health, and disease are, first, the availability and accessibility of food and water; and, second, the safety of food and water for human consumption.

Food Availability and Access

Because most models of global warming predict that the earth will undergo climatic changes that include overall warmer temperatures, changing rain patterns (including both drought and excessive rain), and shifts in growing seasons, it is inevitable that farmers around the world will have to learn to live with the new realities of the climate. Daniel J. Weiss, senior fellow and director of climate strategy at the American Progress Foundation, and researcher Robin Pam state, "Rising temperatures and varying rainfall patterns could affect staple crop production and food security, while aiding the migration and breeding of pests that can devastate crops."[1] Thus, depending on where he or she may live, the farmer of the near future may find longer or shorter growing seasons; more or less rain; and more insects, plant diseases,

Global Warming Causes Malnutrition

Yewande Aramide Awe, a senior environmental engineer with the World Bank in Washington DC, estimates that up to 9% of the GDP [gross domestic product] of several countries in sub-Saharan Africa and South Asia is lost due to the effects of malnutrition. . . .

"Half of the nutritional problems are due to climate change. When there is not enough food to eat, the body is more prone to infection and it's the most pronounced in children. It's a direct vicious cycle between malnutrition and infection. As water becomes scarcer the likelihood of infectious diseases increases."

She says sanitation, water and hygiene become crucial factors in reducing morbidity and mortality. For every death prevented through an environmental health intervention, several additional deaths from other diseases are prevented.

SOURCE: Chris Bateman, "Climate Change Kills at Least 300,000 Every Year," *South African Medical Journal*, October 10, 2009, pp. 20–22.

molds, and fungi. In short, agriculture must change if it is to provide sufficient food to the world's population and maintain the population's health.

In some places, global warming may benefit agriculture. With abundant rain and longer growing seasons, farmers in the higher latitudes may see increases in crop yields. Weiss and Pam suggest, for example, that "cold climate nations, such as Canada, may expand their arable land."[2] Furthermore, as science writer Sarah DeWeerdt asserts:

Some relatively wealthy countries in temperate regions will likely see crop yields rise, mainly due to longer, warmer growing seasons. Even the excess of carbon dioxide in the air that is the underlying cause of climate change can theoretically be a boon for agriculture, acting as a fertilizer when other conditions for plant growth are favorable.[3]

In other areas, however, longer periods of hot weather with inadequate rain will surely lead to crop failures and low yield. In addition, in areas where excessive rain is likely to fall as a result of global warming, crops may be wiped out completely. According to at least one researcher, it may not take extreme weather to seriously affect crop yields, but simply small changes wrought by global warming, including modest temperature and growing season shifts. Brian Halweil, senior researcher at the World Watch Institute argues, "The most serious threats to agriculture will not be the most dramatic: lethal heat wave or severe drought or endless deluge. Instead, for plants that humans have bred to thrive in specific climate conditions, it is those subtle shifts in temperatures and rainfall during key periods in the crops' lifecycles that will be the most disruptive." Halweil points out further that even in the present day, "crop losses associated with background climate variability are significantly higher than those caused by disasters such as hurricanes or flooding."[4]

> *"[Malnutrition] is globally the most important risk factor for illness and death, with hundreds of millions of pregnant women and young children particularly affected."*

Many of the poorest countries in the world are unlikely to reap the benefits of global warming and are much more likely to find their crops inadequate to feed their populations. "Most climatologists agree," writes Halweil, "climate change will hit farmers in the developing world hardest. . . . Farmers in the tropics already find themselves near the temperature limits for most major crops, so any warming is likely to push their crops over the top."[5] Large sections of Africa, for example, are already feeling the effects of global warming–driven temperature changes, droughts, and desertification; it will not take a great deal more warming to make these areas unable to sustain agriculture. Such shifts in the climate set the stage for famine, with all the concurrent health issues that famine brings, including death by starvation.

Food, Health, and Disease

In terms of food availability and access, there are three major areas of health concern. First, when food is not easily available or accessible—because of crop failures, high prices, or conflict— humans suffer from malnutrition. They quickly lose weight, be- cause the intake of calories is not sufficient to sustain body mass. Chronic hunger can damage all systems of the body, including the muscles, nerves, and circulation. In addition, the malnour- ished endure diseases that result from an inadequate intake of vital minerals and nutrients. Indeed, as Olaf Müller from the De- partment of Tropical Hygiene and Public Health at Heidelberg University and Michael Krawinkel of the Institute for Nutritional Sciences of Justus Liebig University-Giessen assert, "Malnutri- tion . . . continues to be a major health burden in developing countries. It is globally the most important risk factor for illness and death, with hundreds of millions of pregnant women and young children particularly affected."[6]

In times of famine, people progressively move from under- nourishment, to malnutrition, to starvation as food becomes less and less available, or disappears altogether. If starvation contin- ues long enough, it leads to death.

A second major concern is that, even if available, food grown on depleted soil may lack the necessary nutrients to sustain hu- man health. For example, people who do not take in enough vi- tamin C are likely to develop scurvy, a disease causing joint pain, rashes, fatigue, and sometimes death. Likewise, a lack of thia- mine, or vitamin B_1, causes beriberi, a disease of the nervous sys- tem that results in fatigue, heart failure, and paralysis. Müller and Krawinkel list iron, iodine, vitamin A, and zinc as the primary deficiencies among the malnourished in developing countries.

A final health problem related to food access is that people who are chronically hungry and malnourished are extremely susceptible to secondary, opportunistic infectious diseases, as well as diseases caused by parasites. Whereas a well-nourished and healthy person might resist malaria, an undernourished person may not have any resistance to the disease. In addition, common illnesses such as influenza may have deadly complications such as pneumonia or encephalitis in people who suffer from malnutrition.

One of the effects of global warming on human health, then, is the potential it has for creating widespread crop failures that eventually could lead to a lack of available food and perhaps even famine, with all the accompanying health problems. Countries will need to establish efficient and effective early warning systems to make themselves able to identify areas and regions where crop failures or environmental disasters could result in food shortages. By identifying these areas early, governments may be able to quickly move resources into place to prevent widespread suffering and death. To do so, of course, governments will also have to have a strong famine preparedness plan that includes stockpiling of resources during good years and identifying other ways to manage shortfalls in food supplies. Finally, in order to sustain food availability and access to ensure the health of their citizens, countries will need to encourage their farmers to find suitable crops to fit the new climatic reality.

The Controversy over Genetically Modified Food

Some scientists believe that genetically modified crops can provide an answer to the challenges global warming places on food availability and accessibility. In the last decades of the twentieth century, scientists learned to manipulate the genetic code, or DNA, of various plants and animals. By splicing the DNA from one organism into the DNA of a second organism, scientists were able to pass a trait from the first organism to the second. For example, a researcher might isolate a gene that prevents mildew and rot in beans and splice it into tomatoes, producing a tomato that looks and tastes just like a traditionally grown tomato, but which is resistant to mildew and rot. Such tomatoes would appeal to consumers and be more profitable for the business that grows them.

On the one hand, such gene-splicing opens a world of possibilities for the improvement of food. Food that is resistant to disease and drought could one day feed the hungry of the world, supporters of genetically modified food argue. Pest-resistant crops are also a possibility. In addition, genetically modified crops often produce larger crop yields, making food less expensive and more available. As Tuskegee Institute genetic food researcher C.S. Prakash argues, "Biotechnology represents a powerful tool that we can employ now in concert with many other traditional approaches in increasing food production in the face of diminishing land and water resources."[7]

On the other hand, opponents fear that genetically modified food might not be safe. They charge that genetic mutations could run amok and damage human health. They also contend that genetically modified crops will destroy traditional agriculture and decrease biodiversity. The seed for such crops can also be very expensive, unaffordable for many poor farmers. In addition, genetically modified seeds are sometimes loaded with a gene that prevents farmers from replanting a second crop from seed derived from the first crop. Thus, the farmer must always buy new seed, rather than using saved seed from previous harvests. The Union of Concerned Scientists lists a number of additional objections to genetically modified food:

- They may introduce new allergens and cause allergic reactions to those who consume them

- They may increase antibiotic resistance in humans who eat the food

- They may introduce new toxins into the environment

Excess atmospheric CO$_2$, as projected by some global warming models, may benefit certain crops, but extreme heat or reduced rain would devastate many others. AP Images.

- They may introduce new viruses
- They may damage wildlife[8]

Thus, while many believe that genetic modification may help resolve some climate change–related agricultural problems, the issue is so controversial that it is unclear whether this course of action will actually increase food security around the world. Whereas in the United States genetically modified foods are quite common, Europeans are much more reluctant to stock such foods in stores. Nations elsewhere share Europe's concerns about genetic modifications. Governments in Africa, for example, have turned away emergency food supplies that included genetically modified foods. At issue is whether policies will ultimately be determined by the need for greater food supplies to combat starvation in famine-stricken areas or by concerns over the safety of genetically modified food.

Water Availability and Access

According to Mark Maslin, director of the Environment Institute at the City College of London, "By far the most important threat to human health . . . is access to fresh drinking water."[9] Fully one-third of the world's population lives in countries that are water stressed, according to Maslin. At the same time, the population of the world continues to grow, and the demand for water for drinking, for irrigation, for watering livestock, and for manufacturing continues to climb. David Archer, writing in his book *Global Warming: Understanding the Forecast*, concurs, stating, "Water availability may be the most important impact of global warming on human welfare."[10]

Global warming will negatively affect freshwater access in several ways. First, in some places there will be *too much* water. For example, during hurricanes and heavy rain events, storm surges and flooding might overwhelm and contaminate freshwater supplies. In addition, river runoff may not only deplete the soil (leading to low yields and crops without adequate nutritional value) but may also contaminate drinking water.

Second, in other areas of the world, climate change is expected to result in reduced rainfall. Many of these areas are already experiencing drought conditions, and increasing areas of the world are becoming ever more arid. In such places, freshwater sources such as lakes and rivers are drying up.

The Soaring Demand for Water

Furthermore, the growing urbanization of the world makes achieving an adequate water supply even more difficult. Cities are largely paved, and, as explained by Eleanor Sterling, director of the Center for Biodiversity and Conservation at the Museum of American History, "As more land is paved over, rainwater can no longer soak into the ground or evaporate slowly to recharge the system."[11] In addition, cities do not generally have an adequate number of trees to absorb rainwater and return it to the ecosystem. Cities also create a heat island effect, wherein urban areas are much hotter than the surrounding areas. Global warming has exacerbated this effect. Rainfall evaporates quickly on hot pavement, rather than replenishing water supplies. At the same time, growing cities also place an increasing demand on freshwater for urban populations. Often, water must be transported through aqueducts and pipelines from remote locations; any breakdown in these systems spells disaster for city residents in need of fresh drinking water.

Coping Strategies for a Thirsty World

It is likely that demand for freshwater will continue to grow in coming years; a warming planet requires even more water for drinking, agriculture, cooling, and industry. As freshwater sources dwindle, however, the world will have to find new ways

---

WATER FACTS AND FIGURES

- Saltwater accounts for 97 percent of all water on earth.

- The Americas have the most freshwater of the continents of earth; Oceania has the least.

- 2 million people, mostly children under age 5, die from illnesses caused by dirty water each year, as estimated in 2009.

- Nearly 6.6 billion people worldwide lack access to a supply of clean water, according to 2009 estimates.

- In 2009, 2.1 billion people lacked basic sanitation facilities.

- By 2025, the United Nations estimates that 2.8 billion people will face freshwater stress or scarcity.

Source: Compiled by author.

to quench its thirst. One possibility is technology that will make desalination plants cost-effective. These plants can take abundant seawater, remove the salt, and make the water safe for drinking, watering livestock, and irrigating crops. Opponents of such plans believe that desalination of seawater is not safe, too expensive, and destructive to the ecosystem of the ocean.

City governments can find ways of increasing the green spaces in urban areas. An increased number of trees and plants would return more water to the ecosystem, provide natural cooling for residents and buildings, and combat the heat island effect. This approach would provide additional health benefits by lowering the number of deaths due to heat waves. In addition, lowering the temperature in a city by increasing green spaces will also reduce ozone formation, thereby decreasing air pollution and the health problems that go along with excessive ozone.

An unpopular, but perhaps necessary, measure that could be taken is water rationing. Across the United States, cities in drought-stricken areas regularly enact ordinances limiting car washing and lawn watering. Additional regulations on water usage could help preserve water supply. Many citizens feel that government should not regulate their lives or their access to water, however.

Most scientists believe that simply reducing the demand for water is a reasonable goal. Sterling reports, "Hydrologists estimate that as much as 60 percent of the water extracted from aquatic systems for human use is simply wasted—lost to leakage, evaporation, inefficient appliances and human carelessness."[12]

Leaders of some countries and states are looking for large quantities of freshwater resources outside their own jurisdictions. For example, some Middle Eastern countries have explored the notion of tugging icebergs from the North Atlantic and Antarctic oceans to their borders to provide freshwater. Governors from the desert states in the American Southwest look toward the Great Lakes as a potential source of freshwater. At the same time, the governors of the Great Lakes states, as well as Canadian provincial leaders, have pledged to protect the waters of the Great Lakes against diversion to other locations.

Clearly, access to both food and water are essential to human health. Even if access could be secured, however, a serious concern would remain: How will global warming affect the safety of food and water for human use?

Food and Water Safety in a Warming World

Global warming is likely to affect not only the quantity of food and water available for the earth's population, but also the quality of that food and water. In *Natural History* magazine, science writer Sharon P. Napper and colleagues point out the threat that diminished access to freshwater places on human lives. She adds: "But consider the condition of the water when it finally trickles down people's throats. Infectious pathogens and harmful chemicals—from parasites to poisons—contaminate the world's freshwater and contribute to the deaths of millions of people worldwide every year."[13] Scientists generally agree that as the climate changes, there will be an increase in illness caused by both food and water, for several reasons.

First, it is expected that climate changes will encourage growing populations of pests, including flies, rodents, and insects such as cockroaches. Some of these pests damage food supplies by eating them; in addition, infestations of bugs make the food inedible or dangerous to eat: infested foods can be a source for infection by parasites, bacteria, and viruses.

Food also rots and spoils much more quickly in warmer temperatures, which encourage bacterial growth. Salmonella, *E. coli*, and other harmful bacteria breed on food that has not been refrigerated properly, something that will be increasingly difficult as temperatures rise.

Many people depend on food from coastal waters, and global warming will also affect the safety of this resource. Brazilian researcher Ulisses Confalonieri and his colleagues note that people have been sickened by contaminated shellfish in the United States, Japan, and Asia. He adds, "A large outbreak [of a diarrheal illness] in 2004 due to the contamination of oysters . . . was linked to atypically high temperatures in Alaskan coastal waters."[14]

Similar troubles affect freshwater resources. Contamination from water-borne pathogens is much more likely during warmer weather. Cities such as Milwaukee, Wisconsin, have had to issue boil orders for residents, requiring them to boil all water from city supplies before cooking, washing, or drinking, in order to protect residents from a diarrhea-causing parasite, cryptosporidium. Walkerton, Ontario, was the site of a tragic disaster when its water supply was tainted with *E. coli* bacteria, leading to the deaths of at least seven people and sickening more than a thousand. In addition, using contaminated water to wash fresh fruits and vegetables can result in serious water-borne illnesses, including typhoid fever.

As the climate warms, then, public health and governmental leaders will need to join forces with the medical community and the general population not only to ensure access to adequate food and water, but also to ensure that these necessities are safe. In warmer temperatures, and with the vagaries of climate change, each individual will need to remain vigilant to protect his or her own health.

Notes

1. Daniel J. Weiss and Robin Pam, "The Human Side of Global Warming," Center for American Progress, April 10, 2008. www.americanprogress.org.
2. Weiss and Pam, "The Human Side of Global Warming."
3. Sarah DeWeerdt, "Climate Change, Coming Home: Global Warming's Effects on Populations," *World Watch*, vol. 20, May-June 2007, pp. 8–13.
4. Brian Halweil, "The Irony of Climate: Archaeologists Suspect That a Shift in the Planet's Climate Thousands of Years Ago Gave Birth to Agriculture. Now Climate Change Could Spell the End of Farming as We Know It," *World Watch*, vol. 18, March-April 2005, pp. 20–21.
5. Brian Halweil, "The Irony of Climate," p. 21.
6. Olaf Müller and Michael Krawinkel, "Malnutrition and Health in Developing Countries," *Canadian Medical Association Journal*, vol. 173, August 2, 2005. www.cmaj.ca.
7. C.S. Prakash, "Genetically Modified Crops Are Good for Africa," *The Vanguard* (Nigeria), February 8, 2005.

8. Union of Concerned Scientists, "Risks of Genetic Engineering," June 6, 2007. www
   .ucsusa.org.
9. Mark Maslin, *Global Warming: A Very Short Introduction*, Oxford: Oxford University
   Press, 2004, p. 95.
10. David Archer, *Global Warming: Understanding the Forecast*, Malden, MA: Blackwell,
    2007, p. 164.
11. Eleanor Sterling, "Blue Planet Blues: Demand for Freshwater Threatens to Outstrip
    Supply. How Can We Meet the Needs of All Earth's Species?" *Natural History*, vol.
    116, November 2007, p. 31.
12. Sterling, "Blue Planet Blues," p. 31.
13. Sharon P. Napper, Robert S. Lawrence, and Kellogg J. Schwab, "Dangerous Waters:
    Twenty Percent of the People on Earth Lack Access to Clean Water. And Even That
    Dismal Number Is Likely to Grow," *Natural History*, vol. 116, November 2007, p. 46.
14. Ulisses Confalonieri, "2007: Human Health," *Climate Change 2007: Impacts, Adapta-
    tion, and Vulnerability. Contribution of Working Group II to the Fourth Assessment
    Report of the Intergovernmental Panel on Climate Change*, eds. M.L. Parry et al. Cam-
    bridge: Cambridge University Press, 2007, p. 400.

CHAPTER 8

Melting Ice and Rising Sea Levels: Impacts on Health

Global warming will drastically affect the lives of millions of people living in coastal areas around the globe in two important, connected, and documented ways: Land-based ice from glaciers and the polar ice sheets is melting, and sea levels are rising. The twin effects of these two events may be devastating for the millions of people living in coastal areas of the world. As the Pew Center on Global Climate Change explains, "Among the most serious and potentially catastrophic effects of climate change is sea-level rise, which is caused by a combination of 'thermal expansion' of ocean water as it warms and the melting of land-based ice."[1] Thermal expansion simply means that as water warms, it increases in volume. Thus, warmer water takes up more space than cooler water and will cause oceans to rise. Land-based ice is freshwater ice found in glaciers or ice sheets over land. Icebergs are also a form of land-based ice, because they are made of freshwater and are caused by chunks of glaciers falling, or calving, into the ocean. When land-based ice melts in the oceans, or when runoff from melting glaciers reaches the sea, the melting ice contributes to an increased volume of seawater, leading to sea-level rise. Melting, free-floating sea ice, formed when ocean saltwater freezes, does not cause ocean levels to rise, because the melted water displaces the same amount of water as what is displaced by the ice. This effect is similar to the way a glass filled with water and ice cubes does not overflow when the ice cubes melt.

Projecting Global Sea Rise

Projections vary for global sea rise. The most commonly quoted figures come from the International Panel on Climate Change's (IPCC) 2007 report in which the panel offered a projection of 23 inches to 35 inches (58 cm to 88.9 cm) of sea-level rise by 2100. Others, however, are much more pessimistic. The Pew Forum's study indicates that by 2100, "if nothing is done to rein in GHG [greenhouse gas] emissions, global sea level could be 2.5 to 6.5 feet (.7 to 1.9 m) higher than it is today, depending on how much land-based ice melts."[2] Of special concern is the ice sheet covering Greenland: Not only does the Greenland ice sheet appear vulnerable, but, should it rapidly disintegrate, it has the potential of raising sea levels dramatically. Stefan Rahmstorf, an ocean physicist at Potsdam University, argues that the complete melting of all earth's ice sheets "would result in a global sea-level

Land-Based Ice, Sea Ice, and Rising Oceans

Much has been made of rising sea levels due to global warming. Often, writers refer to ice melt as an important factor in the rise of the seas. It is important, however, to distinguish between two different kinds of ice, land-based ice and sea ice. Land-based ice is composed of freshwater. As its name suggests, it is ice that begins on land, not in the sea. For example, glaciers that form amid mountains are a type of land-based ice. Likewise, the Greenland ice sheet, a vast body of ice that covers more than 80 percent of that country, is an example of land-based ice. Sea ice, on the other hand, is composed of saltwater. It is formed by the freezing of seawater in frigid polar regions. Much of the so-called land of the Arctic region is not land at all, but rather solidly frozen sea ice (which is in contrast to Antarctica, a continental landmass under large quantities of ice).

rise of about 70 m [about 229 feet]."[3] To be clear, Rahmstorf does not project that this will happen; he does believe that it is likely the world will witness a sea-level rise of more than 3 feet (.9 m) by 2100, however, based on the relationship between sea-level rise and temperature that has held true for the past century.

Some researchers suggest a much more modest sea-level rise, however, or doubt that sea levels will rise at all. A study led by W.T. Pfeffer of the Institute of Arctic and Alpine Research, University of Colorado, concludes that sea-level rise will *not* be as great as predicted. The team writes,

> We conclude that increases in excess of 2 meters are physically untenable. We find that a total sea-level rise of about 2 meters by 2100 could occur under physically possible glaciological conditions, but only if all variables are quickly accelerated to

Global warming is causing both land-based ice and sea ice to melt. The melting of land-based ice can cause ocean levels to rise, with all the health hazards this represents, including flooding and saltwater incursion into freshwater supplies. The water released from the melting of land-based ice increases the total volume of the ocean.

Melting sea ice, though, does *not* contribute to rising sea levels. This is because the sea ice is already a part of the total volume of the ocean. When sea ice is in a frozen state, it displaces exactly the same amount of water as it does once it melts.

Although melting sea ice does not pose a hazard for rising sea levels, it does seriously affect the health of the indigenous peoples of the Arctic region. They live much of their lives on sea ice, and their traditional forms of hunting are all carried out on sea ice. When ice becomes unstable through melting, it becomes dangerous for both humans and their traditional prey. In addition, sea ice reflects heat, thus contributing to the cooling of the Arctic environment. As it melts, however, there is more dark, open water. The dark water absorbs heat, raising the temperature of ocean waters, in turn increasing the melting of ice.

extremely high limits. More plausible but still accelerated conditions lead to total sea-level rise by 2100 of about 0.8 meter.[4]

Of course, it should be noted that even a rise of 0.8 meters places the sea levels at about 2.6 feet, or 30 inches (76 cm), over their current levels. For low-lying areas, this can be a very crucial difference: 30 inches of water permanently flowing through a home makes the house unlivable. And growing crops under 30 inches of seawater is impossible.

The Past Offers a Clue to the Present

Some scientists are looking to the past to relate the amount of carbon dioxide (CO_2) in the atmosphere to times in Earth's history when there has been a similar amount of atmospheric CO_2, a potent greenhouse gas thought to be driving global warming. University of California, Los Angeles, assistant professor Aradhna Tipati is the lead author in a study with startling results: It demonstrates that the last time carbon dioxide levels were as high as they were in 2009 was 15 million years ago. She notes, "The last time carbon dioxide levels were apparently as high as they are today, global temperatures were 5 to 10 degrees Fahrenheit higher than they are today, the sea level was approximately 75 to 120 feet higher than today, there was no permanent sea ice cap in the Arctic and very little ice on Antarctica and Greenland."[5]

In 2008 the United Nations Environment Program projected that 80 percent of the world's population would live within 62 miles (99.8 km) of a coastline, and a full 40 percent would live just 37 miles (59.6 km) from the coast by 2010.

Another group of researchers led by University of Wisconsin paleoclimatologist Anders Carlson found evidence that the glaciers that stretched over Canada and the Great Lakes region of the United States melted very quickly. These glaciers, known as the Laurentide ice sheet, completely disappeared "in two geologically rapid bursts, shedding enough ice to raise sea levels by as much as four feet per century,"[6] according to a summary of Carlson's study by David Biello in *Scientific American*. Such research does not suggest that the same will happen in the near future, but rather that such melting can happen, and can happen quickly.

Coastal Areas Are Densely Populated and at Risk

Obviously, trying to put an exact figure on what can be expected in terms of sea-level rise is difficult, if not impossible. It is entirely possible to document that sea levels have been rising over the past century, however, and that there is no reason to doubt that they will continue to rise as temperatures warm and land-ice melts. Because one-third to one-half of the world's population lives in coastal areas (and that number is growing), any rise of current ocean levels exacerbates the health risks these people are already recognizing. In 2008 the United Nations Environment Program projected that 80 percent of the world's population would live within 62 miles (99.8 km) of a coastline, and a full 40 percent would live just 37 miles (59.6 km) from the coast by 2010.

As the ocean rises, coastal areas are in danger of flooding, and barrier islands will be more dramatically affected by ocean overwash during storms. A small hurricane with a storm surge of just 5 feet to 8 feet (1.5 m to 2.4 m), for example, can be deadly when an area is barely above sea level, as is much of the populated area of Bangladesh, for example. Likewise, low-lying barrier islands along coastlines can be completely overwashed when waves caused by high winds top dunes or protective dikes, causing serious erosion and damage. Some of the world's poorest peoples live in coastal megacities, and their houses are unlikely to withstand such surges or overwash.

Cyclone Nargis is a case in point. A year after the May 2, 2008, disaster, the *New York Times* reported that an estimated eight-five thousand people died as a result of Cyclone Nargis in the Southeast Asian nation of Myanmar; another fifty-four thousand people were listed as still missing at that time. Many were swept away by a storm surge that flooded the low-lying Irrawaddy Delta. The damage was made worse by high sea levels and by high population density in the coastal areas. Some seven hundred thousand people lost their homes in this storm, according to the *New York Times*, and still more suffered serious health effects such as cholera, parasitic infection, and other diarrheal diseases. Again, because so many of the most densely populated places in the world are on coastlines, storm surges coupled with rising sea levels will affect millions of people.

The Health Risks of Seawater Incursion

Rising sea levels can also cause an incursion of seawater into low-lying coast areas. Once saltwater seeps into coastal soil, it makes the land unfit for growing crops, as saltwater will kill most plants. In addition, saltwater is not drinkable. When ocean flooding occurs, it often destroys freshwater resources such as wells, lakes, rivers, and city water systems. People living in these areas are likely to suffer from a lack of access to freshwater as a result. The Centers for Disease Control and Prevention notes that "saltwater entering freshwater drinking supplies is a . . . concern for these regions and increased salt content in soil can hinder agricultural activity in coastal areas."[7]

In addition, when ocean levels become higher than the level of rivers running into the ocean, the river current can reverse. In these cases, a large quantity of saltwater runs from the ocean upstream, turning freshwater into saltwater or brackish water. Because freshwater fish cannot live in seawater, there follows a large kill-off of river life, an important source of food for people who live on riverbanks. Furthermore, the river water can no longer be used for irrigating crops.

A joint team of Japanese and Vietnamese researchers studied this problem in the Mekong Delta of Vietnam, a low-lying

coastal area responsible for 50 percent of that nation's rice production and more than 80 percent of its rice for export. They
note, "This high level of rice production is dependent upon the
abundance of freshwater from the Mekong River. . . . Salinity intrusion is a major constraint to the irrigation planning initiatives
for rice cultivation in the delta." They concluded that a large sec-
tion of this important rice-producing region will be negatively
impacted by "two of the most ascertained consequences of climate change—sea-level rise and the reduction of the Mekong
River in the dry season."[8]

One critical impact, then, of saltwater incursion into low-
lying coastal lands is that it can lead to food and water shortages, potentially leading to malnutrition, dehydration, and the
accompanying health problems associated with them. Malnutrition and dehydration leave people vulnerable to a host of additional infections, including attack by viruses, bacteria, and
parasites. Tellingly, Mark Maslin, director of the Environment
Institute of the Department of Geography at University College
London, notes, "There is a strong correlation between increased
sea-surface temperature and sea level and the annual severity of
the cholera epidemics in Bangladesh."[9]

Losing Homes to Rising Seas

Finally, rising sea levels will totally inundate some areas, forcing
people to leave their homes and countries. In addition, a number of island nations will cease to exist if even low-end estimates
are accurate. The Maldives, for example, an island nation of 200
inhabited islands and more than 1,100 islets, is at extreme risk:
More than 80 percent of the Maldives is just 3.2 feet to 4.9 feet
(1 m to 1.5 m) above sea level, according to the Central Intelli-
gence Agency *Fact Book*, and the highest point in the country is
just 7.8 feet (2.4 m) above sea level.

People who are forced to temporarily leave their homes face
overcrowded conditions, food and water shortages, and exposure
to dangerous illnesses in makeshift refugee camps. All who then

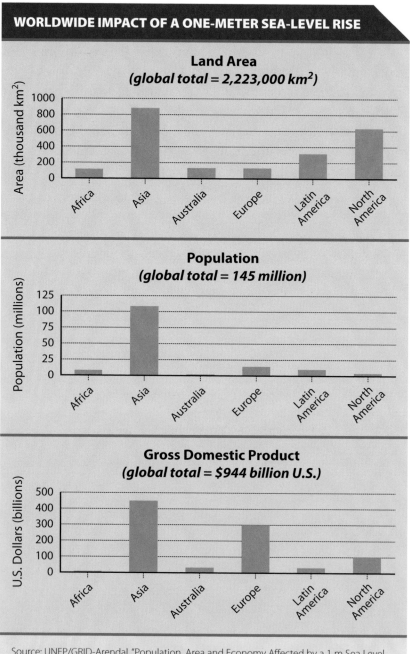

WORLDWIDE IMPACT OF A ONE-METER SEA-LEVEL RISE

Land Area
(global total = 2,223,000 km²)

Area (thousand km²)

Africa | Asia | Australia | Europe | Latin America | North America

Population
(global total = 145 million)

Population (millions)

Africa | Asia | Australia | Europe | Latin America | North America

Gross Domestic Product
(global total = $944 billion U.S.)

U.S. Dollars (billions)

Africa | Asia | Australia | Europe | Latin America | North America

Source: UNEP/GRID-Arendal, "Population, Area and Economy Affected by a 1 m Sea Level Rise (Global and Regional Estimates, Based on Today's Situation)," UNEP/GRID-Arendal Maps and Graphics Library, 2007. www.grida.no.

must find new housing suffer the additional burden incurred by a sudden loss of livelihood and home. Mental health issues are also problematic for environmental refugees and migrants, as noted by the organization Physicians for Social Responsibility. Presently, the world has little mechanism for handling the special health needs of people whose homes and homelands have disappeared. It is a matter that must be considered in the coming years. As secretary general of the United Nations Kofi Annan said in addressing the Global Humanitarian Forum in 2009:

> How will we give longer-term protection to those forced to leave their land and communities due to climate change? The number of displaced people is set to grow. Their plight is as great—and more permanent—than those forced to flee conflict or persecution. But they have no protection under international law.[10]

Rising Sea Levels, Melting Ice, and Indigenous Arctic Peoples

Global warming also threatens the health and homes of indigenous Arctic peoples due to rising sea levels and melting sea ice. These peoples live in areas that may be destroyed by rising waters, forcing them to relocate. In addition, warm seawaters are melting floating sea ice. Although the melting sea ice is not thought to contribute to rising sea levels, it does pose serious health risks to native peoples. They risk drowning while hunting or fishing on sea ice that can break away from the main ice sheet or that has melted through in some areas. In addition, their traditional food sources, including polar bears and seals, are endangered because of loss of habitat. Polar bears are at special risk. The bears spend the winter and spring hunting on sea ice; however, because sea ice is melting earlier and refreezing later in the year due to warming temperatures, the period during which the bears can hunt is reduced. It is crucial to their survival that they are well-nourished during the hunting season, as they must live off their

Scientists fear that water from melting glaciers in Iceland and elsewhere will contribute to a rise in sea levels. Marcel Mochet/AFP/Getty Images.

accumulated body fat through the summer when they stay on land, away from the prey that sustains them. Mother polar bears are particularly vulnerable, as they must not only sustain themselves through this time, they must also nurse their young. Without adequate fat storage, neither mother nor cubs can survive.

Traditional food preparation and consumption also becomes more dangerous for indigenous peoples as the temperature warms and the ice melts. In warming temperatures, meat does not stay hard frozen, but rather can partially thaw and then refreeze, thereby allowing for the growth of sometimes dangerous bacteria. In addition, warming seawaters provide an environment that is favorable to the growth and proliferation of the bacteria that cause botulism, a serious and often fatal form of food poisoning. The diet of the indigenous Arctic peoples puts them at special risk for this dangerous disease. According to CDC researcher Joseph B. McLaughlin and his colleagues,

The incidence of botulism in Alaska is among the highest in the world, and all cases of foodborne botulism in Alaska have been associated with eating traditional Alaskan native foods, including "fermented" foods, dried foods, seal oil and muk-tuk (skin and a thin pinkish blubber layer immediately underneath the skin) from marine mammals.[11]

Eventually, melting ice could lead to relocation for many Arctic people. Many studies demonstrate that indigenous peoples who are forced to migrate end up in urban environments, where their health suffers. Researchers Jo Woodman and Sophie Grig document that indigenous peoples who have been dispossessed of their lands suffer from higher mortality rates, lower life expectancy, and more health problems than those groups who have been able to remain on their land.[12] Alcoholism and mental health issues lead an alarming number of native peoples to take their own lives after they are forced to move out of their traditional environment. Indeed, much of the Inuit and other arctic indigenous cultures are at risk of extinction because of global warming. Franklyn Griffiths, a retired University of Toronto professor and expert on the Arctic, put it bluntly in a recent interview, stating that Inuit culture will disappear with the disappearance of their hunting grounds because of climate change. "There's a cultural genocide implied. . . . They won't be able to practice a hunting culture at all."[13]

Coping with Rising Seas

In the developed countries of the world, work is already under way to plan and prepare for rising sea levels. The Dutch Delta Commission issued a comprehensive report and set of recommendations, for example, as to how the Netherlands, a low-lying coastal European country, will withstand sea rise, floods, and river variations for the next two centuries. They are preparing for a rise of 12 feet (3.6 m) over the next two hundred years, a rise that would put their entire country (already partially below sea level) under water. In the United States, the Army Corps of Engineers is working to rebuild the banks and dams, called levees in Louisiana, that run alongside rivers and that were damaged in 2005 by Hurricane Katrina. The corps seeks to prevent further flooding and seawater incursion into New Orleans.

It will take the concerted effort of both the developing world and the developed world to effectively protect the millions of poor people living in coastal areas, however, and particularly in the megacities of Asia. Teams of medical and emergency personnel must be ready to respond to catastrophes caused by sea-level rise. Engineers, physicists, and planners must work to provide adequate infrastructure to ensure safe water, adequate food, and flood-resistant housing. In addition, the nations of the world must work together to identify how best to help those nations whose homelands are sinking beneath the sea.

Notes

1. "Climate Change 101: Science and Impacts," *Climate Change 101: Understanding and Responding to Global Climate Change*, Pew Center on Global Climate Change, January 2009. www.pewclimate.org.
2. "Climate Change 101," Pew Center on Global Climate Change.
3. Stefan Rahmstorf, "A Semi-Empirical Approach to Projecting Future Sea-Level Rise," *Science*, vol. 315, January 19, 2007, p. 368.
4. W.T. Pfeffer, J.T. Harper, S. O'Neal, "Kinematic Constraints on Glacier Contributions to 21st-Century Sea-Level Rise," *Science*, vol. 321, September 5, 2008, p. 1340.
5. Quoted in Stuart Wolpert, "Last Time Carbon Dioxide Levels Were This High: 15 Million Years Ago, Scientists Report," *UCLA News Room*, October 8, 2009. newsroom.ucla.edu.
6. David Biello, "A Deep Thaw: How Much Will Vanishing Glaciers Raise Sea Levels? Some Say High, Some Say Low, Some Say Fast, Some Say Slow," *Scientific American*, September 5, 2008. www.scientificamerican.com.
7. "Health Effects," *Climate Change and Health Effects*, U.S. Centers for Disease Control and Prevention, 2009. www.cdc.gov.
8. Nguyen Duy Khang, Akihiko Kotera, Toshihiro Sakamoto, and Masayuki Yokozawa, "Sensitivity of Salinity Intrusion to Sea Level Rise and River Flow in Vietnamese Mekong Delta—Impacts on Availability of Irrigation Water for Rice Cropping," *Journal of Agricultural Meteorology*, vol. 64, May 2008, pp. 167, 174.
9. Mark Maslin, *Global Warming: A Very Short Introduction*, Oxford: Oxford University Press, 2004, p. 96.
10. Kofi Annan, "Message from the President," *2009 Forum: Human Impact of Climate Change*, June 23–24, 2009. www.ghf-geneva.org.

11. Joseph B. McLaughlin et al., "Botulism Type E Outbreak Associated with Eating a Beached Whale, Alaska," *Emerging Infectious Diseases*, vol. 10, September 2004, p. 1685.

12. Jo Woodman and Sophie Grig, *Progress Can Kill*, London: Survival International, 2007, pp. 10–21.

13. "Canada Inuit Facing 'Cultural Genocide,' Says Arctic Expert," Canwest News Service, November 23, 2007. www.canada.com.

CHAPTER 9

The Impact of Global Warming on Health: Conclusion

The health threats of global warming are challenging, well documented, and already evident. According to the Global Humanitarian Forum, global warming causes about 300,000 deaths worldwide and about $125 billion dollars in loss annually.

As the previous chapters demonstrate, analyzing the impact of global warming on health and disease, nevertheless, is a complicated and sometimes controversial process. Most researchers and scientists agree that threats to public health are likely to emerge in several major categories:

- Direct temperature effects caused by heat and heat waves
- Drought and problems caused by aridity, including desertification and wildfires
- Extreme weather, including hurricanes and heavy rainfalls leading to flooding, landslides, and mud slides
- Degradation of air quality, including ozone, smog, toxic emissions, and increasing levels of aero-allergens, such as pollen, mold, and fungi
- Increased vulnerability to infectious diseases
- Availability and safety of food and freshwater
- Rising sea levels and melting ice

Not all scientists and medical researchers agree as to the severity or the extent of each of the threats listed above, however. In addition, there is controversy over how many health risks can be attributed directly to global warming, as each category is affected by many contributing factors. For example, an extreme weather event such as a hurricane may cause flooding, directly causing death and injury by drowning. The indirect health threats are much more wide ranging, however, and include food shortages, contaminated freshwater sources, forced evacuation and loss of homes, epidemic diseases such as cholera, increases in disease vectors such as malarial mosquitoes, depression and mental health issues, and so on. How seriously each of these factors affects human health is also dependent on many variables, including governmental responses, personal preparedness, economic resources, and political systems in the affected area.

The Young and the Old Are at Risk

Although climate change will affect the health of everyone, it will not do so equally. Some citizens of the world will suffer more deeply than others. Children, for example, are more vulnerable to the health implications of global warming than are adults, for several reasons. First, they must depend on the adults in their lives to plan and prepare for disaster. If adults fail in this important task, children will suffer. Children are often injured in extreme weather events, and sometimes suffer traumatic stress disorder in the aftermath. Furthermore, children and infants are still growing, and their lungs are more vulnerable to the effects of ozone and other forms of pollution. Children will also have to bear the consequences of their parents', grandparents', and great-grandparents' environmental decisions.

The elderly are another highly vulnerable population and are likely to bear more than their share of the negative health impact of global warming. More elderly people die from heat-related distress than any other subgroup. Often, the elderly live alone and do not have the support they need to prepare for or survive extreme weather, heat, or drought. They often have preexisting pulmonary or cardiovascular disease, which is worsened by air pollution. The elderly are also the most likely to die from infectious diseases, because their immune systems do not protect the aged as fully as when they were young. Their physical frailty may prevent them from obtaining safe food and water, which may be in short supply from the effects of global warming.

Poor People and Poor Countries Suffer the Most

The economically disadvantaged form another vulnerable population. Poor people rarely have the means to cool themselves during heat waves and may suffer more heat stroke. They often live in urban areas where heat intensities are magnified. Around the globe, many of the poorest people live in high-risk coastal areas that are subject to flooding from rising ocean levels and strong storms. Many others live in rural areas that suffer from drought and may find it difficult to get food or water. They are often unable to afford high prices when weather events create shortages, and often, their physical condition is already weakened by malnutrition and disease. They are also the most likely to find themselves environmental refugees, forced from their homes by drought, floods, rising seas, or melting ice.

Eight of the warmest years since records have been kept were in the first decade of the twenty-first century.

Poor countries do not have the public health infrastructure to adequately protect their populations from the health threats of global warming. In addition, many of the poorest countries are also in the geographical locations that stand to receive the brunt of global warming's challenges. Bangladesh, for example, is located in low-lying land around a river delta subject to flooding from sea rise and also to storm surges from tropical cyclones. Ethiopia chronically suffers from drought and desertification, and consequently from food and water shortages.

What Is the IPCC?

The Intergovernmental Panel on Climate Change (IPCC) is the world's leading authority on climate change. Established in 1988 by the World Meteorological Organization (WMO) and the United Nations Environment Programme (UNEP), the purpose of the IPCC is to pool, evaluate, and summarize the state of scientific knowledge about all aspects of climate change, especially human-caused climate change, and to evaluate policies related to climate change.

The IPCC shared the Nobel Peace Prize in 2007 with climate-change activist and former U.S. Vice President Al Gore. The Nobel Committee acknowledged the work of both prizewinners in bringing awareness of climate change to people throughout the world.

The IPCC does not conduct original research, but is a forum for developing a consensus view on climate change issues. Experts are appointed to the IPCC by each participating government. The scientists work as volunteers. IPCC reports are prepared following a complex process in which authors prepare a draft that is peer-reviewed, revised, reviewed by experts and the participating governments, and revised again to produce a final draft that is again reviewed by participating governments. The IPCC's reports are some of the most intensively peer-reviewed summaries of scientific knowledge ever produced.

SOURCE: "Intergovernmental Panel on Climate Change (IPCC)." *Global Issues in Context Online Collection*. Detroit: Gale, 2009. http://find.gale-group.com/gic/start.do?prodId=GIC.

United Nations secretary-general and president of the Global Humanitarian Forum Kofi Annan sums up the challenges of climate change thus:

Climate change is a grave and all-encompassing threat—to our health, our security, our prosperity and quality of life. Climate change is affecting every continent and accelerating faster than previously had been thought. And it is having a catastrophic impact on the lives of millions of people. It is the poorest countries and poorest people who are, and will, suffer most.[1]

Mitigation and Adaptation

There are at least two major schools of thought concerning how to address the health threats of global warming. First, there are those who believe that the health risks of global warming can be addressed only by mitigating global warming itself through the reduction of greenhouse gases. They believe that slowing, or stopping, the warming process is the best way to protect human health.

Others, however, argue that focusing on how the world's populations should adapt to global warming, and how to cope with its concomitant health problems, is a better strategy for public health. Indur M. Goklany, an electrical engineer, is the author of several books about global warming. He writes, "Global health would be advanced farther, faster, more surely, and more economically if efforts are focused not on reducing greenhouse gas emissions, but on reducing vulnerability to today's urgent health problems that may be exacerbated by global warming."[2]

Most agree that the first effects of global warming have already begun. Eight of the warmest years since records have been kept were in the first decade of the twenty-first century. Sea levels are rising. Ozone action days, declared by the U.S. Environmental Protection Agency when air pollution reaches dangerous levels, are increasing. Dengue fever and malaria are expanding northward. Fierce storms batter coastlines. Therefore, even if global emissions were drastically reduced immediately, it would be decades or longer before any relief would be felt. But many opportunities exist to improve public health and disaster preparedness to cope with the worst risks. As the Global Humanitarian Forum asserts, "Adapting to climate change is possible up until land is rendered uninhabitable through sea-level rise and flooding, or severe water stress and desertification. . . . While entire nations may disappear, much can be done to protect the lives and livelihoods of the majority of people living in marginal regions afflicted by climate change."[3] Only by working together and planning ahead will all the nations of the world find the means to protect their populations from the impact of global warming on human health and disease.

Notes

1. Kofi Annan, "Message from the President," *2009 Forum: Human Impact of Climate Change*, June 23–24, 2009. www.ghf-geneva.org.
2. Indur M. Goklany, "Global Health Threats: Global Warming in Perspective," *Journal of American Physicians and Surgeons*, vol. 13, Fall 2009, p. 69.
3. "Climate Change and Displacement of People," Global Humanitarian Forum, June 23–24, 2009. www.ghf-geneva.org.

Glossary

aero-allergen Any airborne substance causing an allergic reaction, such as pollen or mold spores.

airborne particulates Particles of matter or droplets of liquid suspended in the air, usually as a result of air pollution.

anthropogenic Caused by humans.

arboviruses Disease-causing viruses carried primarily by arthropods such as ticks, mosquitoes, or sand flies, though also found in some bats and rodents.

carbon dioxide (CO_2) A greenhouse gas chemically composed of carbon and oxygen. Carbon dioxide is produced by the burning of fossil fuels such as oil and coal. It is also exhaled by human beings and inhaled by plants. Burning plants also release carbon dioxide.

continental climates Climates that are relatively cold in winter and hot in summer; usually found at the interiors of continents.

desertification The gradual process of habitable land turning into desert as a result of climate change or poor farming practices.

drought A long period of abnormally low rainfall, especially one that affects growing or living conditions.

El Niño A periodic oceanic warming, which can have major effects on weather.

famine Extreme scarcity of food.

feedback loop A process in which one condition creates other conditions that reinforce the first.

food-borne illness Disease that typically follows the consumption of food contaminated with microorganisms such as salmonella or *E. coli* bacteria.

glacier A mass of ice that is located year-round on, and moves over, land.

global warming The increase in the average temperature of the earth's surface and oceans. Global warming has been occurring since the mid-twentieth century and is expected to continue because of the greenhouse effect.

greenhouse effect The heating of the surface of the earth due to the presence of gases that trap energy from the sun.

greenhouse gases Substances that contribute to the greenhouse effect and global warming. Carbon dioxide, methane, and water vapor are all greenhouse gases.

groundwater Water located underneath the ground, either in porous soil or in spaces in rock.

heat wave A prolonged period of abnormally hot weather.

Hurricane Katrina The 2005 storm that devastated the city of New Orleans.

hypothermia The condition of having a dangerously low body temperature, usually caused by exposure to cold temperatures; can lead to death.

ice sheet A mass of glacial ice more than 20,000 square miles (50,000 square kilometers) in area.

ice shelf A floating platform of ice that forms at the junction of a glacier and a coastline.

Intergovernmental Panel on Climate Change (IPCC) A scientific body established by the United Nations to evaluate the risk of climate change caused by human activity.

jet stream Fast flowing, narrow air currents in the atmosphere.

monsoons Seasonal winds, which often have a profound effect on seasonal precipitation.

morbidity rate The incidence of a particular disease or disorder in a given population.

mortality rate The number of deaths in a given area or period, or from a particular cause.

North Atlantic Current An important ocean current in the Atlantic that moves warm surface waters from the equator north toward the Arctic, then sinks down and pulls cold water back toward the equator.

ozone A gas consisting of three oxygen atoms. In the stratosphere, ozone protects the earth from harmful radiation; in the troposphere, ozone is a dangerous pollutant causing serious human illness and distress.

seawater incursion Occurs when storms or floods cause seawater to fill rivers, lakes, and freshwater reservoirs with saltwater, making the water undrinkable and unusable for irrigation.

smog A combination of smoke, particulates, and fog.

snowpack Naturally formed compressed snow. It is especially common in mountainous regions, and it often melts in springtime.

storm surge A rapid rise in offshore ocean water, resulting in shoreline flooding and occurring during a tropical cyclone or hurricane; caused by high winds pushing water toward shore, combined with an ocean-level rise due to low atmospheric pressure at the storm center.

thermal expansion The increase in volume of matter caused by an increase in temperature. Thermal expansion of ocean water as a result of global warming is believed to be one of the major short-term causes of sea-level rise.

ultraviolet radiation Invisible rays that are part of the energy from the sun; can cause sunburn and various kinds of skin cancer.

urban heat island A metropolitan area that is significantly warmer than surrounding rural areas because of the increase of paved surfaces and buildings that absorb heat rather than reflect it.

vector-borne disease Infectious illness caused by the bite of another organism, such as a tick or mosquito.

water-borne illness Disease caused by exposure to or consumption of water contaminated by pathogenic microorganisms.

wetlands Areas of land whose soil is saturated with moisture, either permanently or seasonally.

zoonotic disease An animal disease, such as rabies, that can be spread to humans.

For Further Research

Books

Hans A. Baer and Merrill Singer, *Global Warming and the Political Ecology of Health: Emerging Crises and Systemic Solutions.* Walnut Creek, CA: Left Coast Press, 2009.
> An important analysis of the significant and critical relationships between global warming and human health, using medical, anthropological, and scientific approaches.

William James Burroughs, *Climate Change: A Multidisciplinary Approach*, 2nd ed. Cambridge: Cambridge University Press, 2007.
> A current and comprehensive overview of climate change and its implications for society, drawing on sound science as well as contemporary debate.

Diarmid Campbell-Lendrum and Roberto Bertollini, *Protecting Health from Climate Change: Global Research Priorities.* Geneva: World Health Organization, 2009.
> Argues that climate change is the biggest risk to human health in the twenty-first century and calls for research to be conducted in specific areas to guide public health policy.

Nat Cotts, *Global Warming & Health.* New York: AlphaHouse, 2008.
> A young adult book exploring the health impact of global warming, including emerging diseases, air quality, food and water, and pollution.

Stephan Faris, *Forecast: The Surprising—and Immediate—Consequences of Climate Change.* New York: Holt, 2009.
> On-the-ground reporting of climate change around the world, including health impacts, by a travel journalist.

Tim F. Flannery, *The Weather Makers: How Man Is Changing the Climate and What It Means for Life on Earth.* New York: Atlantic Monthly, 2005.

Argues that humans are changing the climate with serious consequences for human health and disease.

Global Warming: The Causes, the Perils, the Politics—and What It Means for You. New York: Time, 2007.
The editors of *Time* magazine investigate many facets of the global warming debate in a well-illustrated book.

Indur M. Goklany, *Improving the State of the World.* Washington, DC: Cato Institute, 2007.
Argues that climate change is not the most serious threat to human health at this time, and that resources should be spent addressing such matters as hunger, sanitation, and disease, rather than the reduction of greenhouse gases.

John Houghton, *Global Warming: The Complete Briefing.* Cambridge: Cambridge University Press, 2009.
Comprehensive overview of the likely impacts of climate change on human life and society, including health and disease.

Michael E. Mann and Lee R. Kump, *Dire Predictions: Understanding Global Warming.* New York: DK, 2008.
Two climate scientists present summaries and explanations of the Intergovernmental Panel on Climate Change in terms accessible to a nonscientific audience, complete with pictures and illustrations.

Anthony J. McMichael, *Climate Change and Human Health: Risks and Responses.* Geneva: World Health Organization, 2003.
Considers public health challenges growing out of climate change, including extreme weather, infectious diseases, ozone depletion, and radiation.

M.L. Parry et al., *Climate Change 2007: Impacts, Adaptation, and Vulnerability.* Cambridge: Cambridge University Press, 2007.
A publication of the Intergovernmental Panel on Climate Change, covering an assessment of the impact of global warming on water resources, food, infectious diseases, and coastal areas.

Ian Plimer, *Heaven and Earth: Global Warming, the Missing Science.* Ballan, Victoria, Australia: Connor Court, 2009.

A highly honored Australian scientist argues that climate change is the result of natural cycles, not human action, and that current thinking on climate change is dominated by politics, not science.

Siegfried Fred Singer and Dennis T. Avery, *Unstoppable Global Warming: Every 1,500 Years*. Lanham, MD: Rowman & Littlefield, 2007.
A. Argues that global warming is an inevitable natural cycle that will not greatly endanger humans.

Mark Jerome Walters, *Six Modern Plagues and How We Are Causing Them*. Washington, DC: Island, 2004.
A discussion of emerging infectious diseases related to human changes to the environment, including global warming.

Periodicals

Chris Bateman, "Climate Change Kills at Least 300,000 Every Year," *South African Medical Journal*, January 2009.

Rebecca Berg, "The Future of Children's Environmental Health: Coping with Global Warming," *Journal of Environmental Health*, October 2008.

Canada and World Backgrounder, "The Plague," October 2007.

Anthee Carassava, "Greece Declares Emergency as Forest Fire Rages," *The New York Times*, August 25, 2007.

Anthee Carassava, "Hints of Relief in European Heat Wave, But More Flooding in Britain," *The New York Times*, July 25, 2007.

Gregg Easterbrook, "Global Warming: Who Loses—and Who Wins? Climate Change in the Next Century (and Beyond) Could Be Enormously Disruptive, Spreading Disease and Sparking Wars," *Atlantic*, April 2007.

Robin Edwards, "Sea Levels: Science and Society," *Progress in Physical Geography*, October 2008.

Erika Engelhaupt, "Climate Change and the Arctic Diet," *Environmental Health Perspectives*, July 2009.

Jeffrey Gettleman, "Lush Land Dries Up, Withering Kenya's Hopes," *The New York Times*, September 8, 2009.

Alan Gomez and Doyle Rice, "Weather Extremes Stalk Each Coast," *USA Today*, June 17, 2009.

Paritosh Kasotia, "The Health Effects of Global Warming: Developing Countries Are the Most Vulnerable," *UN Chronicle*, June 2007.

Jane Lloyd, "The Link Between Environment and Disease," *UN Chronicle*, March–May, 2006.

Ian Lowe, "Climate Change and Bushfires: The Science, the Facts, the Warnings," *Habitat Australia*, April 2009.

James MacIntyre, "The Gathering Storm: Climate Change Hits the Poorest People Hardest," *New Statesman*, September 21, 2009.

Mercedes Pascual and Menno J. Bouma, "Do Rising Temperatures Matter?" *Ecology*, April 1, 2009.

Janet Pelley, "Will Global Climate Change Worsen Infectious Diseases?" *Environmental Science and Technology*, March 15, 2005.

Andrew C. Revkin, "Study Finds Past Mega-Droughts in Africa," *The New York Times*, April 17, 2009.

Elisabeth Rosenthal, "Likely Spread of Deserts to Fertile Land Requires Quick Response, U.N. Report Says," *The New York Times*, June 28, 2007.

Andrew Saxon and David Diaz-Sanchez, "Air Pollution and Allergy: You Are What You Breathe," *Nature*, March 2005.

Charles W. Schmidt, "Beyond Mitigation: Planning for Climate Change and Adaptation," *Environmental Health Perspectives*, July 2009.

Virginia A. Sharpe, "'Clean' Nuclear Energy? Global Warming, Public Health, and Justice," *The Hastings Center Report*, February 12, 2009.

Space Daily, "Global Warming and Your Health," October 24, 2006.

Space Daily, "Toll of Climate Change on World Food Supply Could Be Worse Than Thought," December 3, 2007.

USA Today, "California Facing Worst Drought in Modern History," January 30, 2009.

Daniel Williams, "The Big Dry," *Time*, May 22, 2008.

Internet Sources

American Geophysical Union, "Damage, Pollution from Wildfires Could Surge as Western U.S. Warms," July 28, 2009. www.agu.org/sci_soc/prrl/2009-22.html.

Environmental Protection Agency, "Ozone: Good Up High Bad Nearby," September 3, 2009. www.epa.gov/oar/oaqps/gooduphigh.

Paul Francuch, "Survey: Scientists Agree Human-Induced Global Warming Is Real, *EurekaAlert*, January 19, 2009. www.eurekalaert.org/pub_releases/2009-01/uoia-ssa011609.php.

Jonathan M. Katz, "Poor Haitians Resort to Eating Dirt," *National Geographic News*, January 30, 2008. http://news.nationalgeographic.com/news/2008/01/080130-AP-haiti-eatin.html.

Matthew McKinnon, ed., "2009 Forum: Human Impact of Climate Change," Global Humanitarian Forum, 2009. www.ghf-geneva.org/OurWork/CreatingDebate/2009Forum/tabid/190/Default.aspx.

Phil Mercer, "Dust Cloud Chokes Eastern Australia," *Voice of America*, September 23, 2009. www.voanews.com/english/2009-09-23-voa12.cfm.

National Aeronautics and Space Administration, "The Ozone We Breathe," October 9, 2009. http://earthobservatory.nasa.gov/Features/OzoneWeBreathe.

National Oceanic and Atmospheric Administration, *El Niño Theme Page*, November 22, 2009. www.pmel.noaa.gov/tao/elnino/nino-home.html.

National Oceanic and Atmospheric Administration, "Global Warming: Frequently Asked Questions," August 20, 2008. www.ncdc.gov/oa/climate/globalwarming.html#q9.

Physicians for Social Responsibility, "The Medical and Public Health Impacts of Global Warming," 2009. www.psr.org/resources/the-medical-and-public-health.html.

ScienceDaily, "Southern California Poses Health Risks to Children," December 4, 2006. www.sciencedaily.com/releases/2006/12/061201105724.htm.

Web Sites

Centers for Disease Control and Prevention (www.cdc.gov). A well-regarded outlet for credible health information from the United States' public health agency.

Environmental Protection Agency (www.epa.gov). This site has a large area devoted exclusively to the health and environmental effects of climate change.

Global Humanitarian Forum (www.ghf-geneva.org). An international foundation dedicated to building global support for environmental and climate justice for all.

Intergovernmental Panel on Climate Change (www.ipcc.ch). Site of the premier organization monitoring global climate change.

National Hurricane Center (www.nhc.noaa.gov). Includes extensive information on the history, dangers, and meteorology of hurricanes, as well as advice for hurricane preparedness.

Physicians for Social Responsibility (www.psr.org). Includes information, research, and many fact sheets on the implications of global warming for human health.

RealClimate: Climate Science from Climate Scientists (www .realclimate.org). An up-to-date commentary site by working climate scientists who provide information for interested members of the public and journalists.

World Health Organization (www.who.int). The public health arm of the United Nations; the site offers a global perspective on the health impacts of global warming.

Index

About the Author

Diane Andrews Henningfeld writes frequently on contemporary issues and literature. She has edited numerous books for Greenhaven Press, including *Opposing Viewpoints: The North and South Poles*, *Global Viewpoints: Famine*, and *At Issue: Do Infectious Diseases Pose a Threat?* A longtime faculty member at Adrian College, Henningfeld holds the rank of professor emerita. In 2009, she hiked the Great Glen Way, a 75-mile trail across Scotland, and she plans to complete the 95-mile West Highland Way in 2010. She lives in Adrian, Michigan, with her husband.